# HOOF PRINTS IN THE SNOW

# HOOF PRINTS IN THE SNOW

## JIM HAWLEY

**To order additional copies of this book, contact:**
Xlibris Corporation
1-888-795-4274
www.Xlibris.com
Orders@Xlibris.com
114464

# ACKNOWLEDGMENTS

I WOULD FIRST and foremost thank my wife for tolerating me during the writing of this story. She has also been indispensable for helping with pictures and computer work. I would also like to thank Nancy Munier for her extensive help in putting the story together. I would like to thank the family of Dr. Edward Howshar, Jennifer Howshar, and Dr. Mark Howshar for giving their permission to use his name in the story.

# CHAPTER 1

THIS IS MY story—although it is really her story. It is a love story, it is a family story, it is a history. I was able to compile it from what I was told by townspeople, the ranchers in the surrounding countryside, local history, local legend, and Lucy Morgan herself.

I am Dr. Jim Holland. I am a country doctor in the small town of Wheatland, Wyoming. Wheatland is located where the Laramie Mountains transition to the great high plains. I've been here for six years now. It has taken almost a year to bring her story together.

I first met Lucy Morgan during my first month of practice in the town. She lived on a small ranch of about six hundred acres just outside town. The ranch was twelve miles northwest of Wheatland. It was on the rising, rolling plain, just southeast of Sheep Mountain. The land was the edge of the prairie, with bumpy hills like very lumpy gravy. The Laramie River flowed through the ranch about fifty yards behind the ranch house. The Laramie River is about eight feet wide and four feet deep in the late spring and about one foot wide and six inches deep by September. The house was situated about one-half mile back off Fletcher

Park Road (to the east) at the end of a gravel driveway. Though she lived on a ranch, the only livestock she owned was an elderly border collie that was going blind named Panda.

A neighboring rancher, Mark Bronson, leased most of the land to run his cattle, which was her only means of income. However, the ranch had been paid off for years, and she owned her twenty-year-old truck outright. So her needs were few.

The first time I saw Lucy was in the office. She was very clean, very pleasant, and very short of breath. Her long forehead had dark age spots burned by the sun. She had deep worry lines on her forehead, indicating years of life's struggles. Around her mouth, her laugh lines were equally as deep, highlighting her love of life. Her short hair was a deep red, but the roots belied a dye job.

I walked into the room with the usual smile on my face. "Good morning, Ms."—I glanced at the chart—"Morgan."

Lucy Morgan snorted softly. "Honey, just call me Lucy, please."

"All right," I replied absentmindedly. I thumbed through her chart. "What can I do for you today?"

"I would really like it if you would perform a miracle and make me twenty again." This time, the smile was real.

"So sorry. I am all out of them. Now tell me what brings you in today." I regretted the wording as soon as I said it.

The twinkle in her eye made me realize that she understood and would let the opening slide without the usual answer that it was a truck that brought her in.

"I am very short of breath," she puffed.

"How long has that been going on?" I asked.

"For the past three days." She leaned forward on the exam table and looked at her bare feet. It is my policy that patients be undressed and placed in a paper gown so that I can do a complete exam. The nurse stood in the corner, making some notes. "My legs have been swelling too."

"Well, let's take a look," I remarked, using the usual doctor's language.

"You go ahead and take a look, hon, I have already seen it." She smiled.

I glanced at the nurse, who was hiding a giggle.

"Very well," I said as I walked to her.

I listened to her heart, which sounded normal. Then I listened to her lungs. The lungs sounded like crinkling paper from the bottom halfway to the top. I listened to her abdomen, which had normal gurgles. I pulled the stethoscope out of my ears and pushed on her abdomen. It was not tender, but by her little giggles, I could tell it was a little ticklish. I then leaned over and pushed on her left leg just to the outside of the tibia (the big bone). The flesh dinted in and remained depressed when I pulled my thumb back. A small amount of light-yellowish-colored fluid filled the depression.

I went to the sink and washed my hands. Then I turned back to Lucy. "I need to send you over to the hospital for some tests."

"What kind of tests?" she inquired.

"Some blood work, an EKG, and an x-ray," I replied.

"The hospital?" questioned Lucy.

"Yes, just across the street," I instructed.

"I know where it is. I was there when they built it!" Lucy snapped.

"Yes, ma'am," I answered sheepishly.

"Then what?" She looked from me to the nurse then back to me. "Do I come back here or wait at the hospital?"

"Wait at the hospital. I will come over and look at it in a bit."

Platte County Memorial Hospital is just across the street from my office. I walk back and forth from the two often.

After seeing two more patients, I trotted to the hospital. Lucy's EKG was unremarkable, but her chest x-ray showed an enlarged heart and fluid in her lungs. Her lab work showed she was in significant heart failure.

I found Lucy waiting in the lobby.

"Ms. Morgan." She gave me a frown. "Lucy, I am afraid you have heart failure and need to be in the hospital for a few days."

"Can't, Doc."

"Why not?"

"Because I have to take care of things at home," she stated simply.

"Your BNP shows you are in significant failure, and it is dangerous to send you home." I raised an eyebrow and gave her my most winning smile.

"What if I don't?" She smiled back.

"You could die."

"I am going to die . . . someday."

She had me. "But I don't want that to be soon." I smirked.

"What do you care?"

I sat down in a chair beside her. "I care because I would like to have some time to get to know you." Not exactly the way it is taught in medical school, but it felt right.

She stared me straight in the eyes for what seemed like forever. "Can I make a phone call?"

"When you get settled in your room, you may use the phone all you want," I replied gently.

"OK" was her only reply.

I went to the nurse and wrote a quick order to admit the woman. I added a few basic orders and hurried back to the office.

At five thirty, I saw the last patient and trudged to the hospital.

I saved Lucy for last. I walked into her room and pulled a chair up beside her bed. I sat and began looking through her chart.

"Aren't you going to say anything?" she quizzed.

I looked up at her. "Sorry." I closed the chart. "How are you feeling?"

"A bit anxious."

"Anxious? Because of your breathing?" I questioned.

"No. Because of Panda," she retorted, looking away.

"Panda?"

She looked back at me. "Panda is my border collie. He's OK outside, but he needs some food put out and his water checked."

"Did you call a neighbor?"

"No one answered."

"Well, I can go by there when I am through here. But you will have to give me directions," I offered.

"No, Doc, I will get someone to take care of him."

I listened to her chest and made a quick note in the chart.

"OK, Lucy, I will be back to see you in the morning." I stood and started out of the room, then stopped. I turned back to her. "You have never had any heart problems before?"

"Just a broken heart . . . but that was years ago."

I shook my head and left.

Hospital day 2 found Lucy breathing better. She had lost twenty pounds of water weight during the night.

I studied her chart before I walked into the room. I tucked the chart under my arm and walked in.

"Well, Lucy, how are you feeling this morning?"

"I feel fine, Doc. When can you spring me from this place?" she quizzed.

"I want to run a few tests. Maybe sometime after lunch I will let you go—if the tests look OK." I quickly examined her. Her lungs sounded clearer. "Did you take care of Panda?"

"Yeah. I finally got hold of Mark Bronson"—she saw my confused look—"the man who leases my pasture for his cattle—and he fed Panda."

"Good." I turned toward the door. "Stay here at least a few more hours, and I'll see you later."

"Can't you stay and talk a bit? Would you like a cup of coffee?"

I turned back to her. "I would love a cup of coffee, but I have several more people to see."

As I left the room, I heard her talking to the nurse. "See, hon, he thinks of them as people and not just patients."

Two lessons learned. Patients are really people, and Lucy calls everyone *hon*.

Mid-October in southeast Wyoming, 2000, was cold and snowy. The small town of Wheatland, Wyoming, was used to wind, cold, and snow.

The usual strep throat was being shared around the schoolhouse, and many older people were sure they were suffering from frostbite. Thus, when I arrived at the office, the exam rooms already had patients and the waiting room was packed.

I finally got to the last morning patient at twelve thirty. I straightened the red plaid tie, which had been pulled askew by two-year-old Josh Seward while I was looking in his throat. I took a deep breath and entered the exam room. There was sour old Mr. Schmidt. He was eighty-four years old and weathered from years in the blistering sun and driving snow. He was over six feet tall with a gray mustache that almost blended into his nose hair. Loose dentures caused his voice to click whenever he talked. His hands were rough and heavily creased with many age spots. They were as large as hams and gnarled with arthritis. When I shook hands with him, his right hand engulfed mine, making it seem to disappear.

Mr. Schmidt had horrible lungs, which was the result of fifty years of smoking nonfiltered cigarettes. But Mr. Schmidt's lungs were not his only problem. In fact, he had a written list. He usually had a written list of his complaints, a list, which I suspect, was compiled mainly by his wife. Usually, I got about 75 percent of his medical history from his wife, and he got very few words in edgewise.

Even though I was getting a little shaky from hunger, I was still able to listen to the liturgy and decided he needed a course of antibiotics and oral prednisone. Still, contrary to his wife's wishes, he was not sick enough to be hospitalized.

When I made it back to my inner sanctum, I found a Subway sandwich and a cola on my desk. I had a whole twenty minutes to eat it. Then I had to return to work on the run.

The afternoon was lighter, so I was finished in the office by four thirty. I trudged to the hospital for evening rounds. Lucy was in her room and fit to be tied.

"Where you been, Doc? I been waitin' all day for you to come and cut me loose," she complained.

"I came as soon as I could." I could almost see the steam coming from her ears.

"Do I get out of this prison today?" she quipped.

I glanced down at her chart, stalling for time. "Not today."

"What! You promised."

"No, I said probably you would get out today." She folded her arms and frowned. "I promise now that you will go home in the morning."

"I'm gonna hold you to it," Lucy commanded.

Her breathing was much better, but her echocardiogram showed that she had had a heart attack sometime in the past. Nothing new, nothing that would require further hospitalization.

"Say, Doc," began Lucy, "Mark is out of town today. Could I impose on you to feed Panda? The food is just inside the door. His dish is on the porch near the door." She smiled. "It won't take you long."

I cocked my head and eyed her. I was tired and hungry but figured it would not take much time. "OK. Draw me a map to your place."

"There's some hay in the barn, which is just behind the house. Could you throw a flake or two out on the ground for the horses?" she wheedled.

"Sure." I shrugged.

"Here." She grinned and handed me a piece of paper with lines on it. "It ain't far from town."

"OK. I will be happy to."

I left her room and returned to the broom closet that the hospital powers-that-be called the doctor's dictation room. I finished up my charting and shrugged on my sheepskin-lined jacket. Turning up the collar, I walked through the snow and cold to my little jeep.

I am unmarried, so I did not have to check in with anyone, but I was getting hungry. I started the jeep and shifted into reverse. Backing out of the parking space, I turned on the windshield wipers to smear the snow, which was still spitting from the darkened sky.

She was right about it not being far from town. I traveled only about twelve miles when I found the turnoff onto her dirt road. I drove half a mile before I was at her house. The road led to the front of the house then turned back upon itself to form a loop. The house was on a rise so that the house was at a higher elevation than the cattle guard. The house itself was split-level with the front of the basement, being above ground and the back buried. The front door, which was actually the top floor, was at ground level while the west end of the house was a story above ground level. At the south end of the top level, there was a deck, which overlooked the Laramie Mountains. I hadn't seen any fences since leaving the highway, but that wasn't unusual. Much of the country around here is open range.

The house was small, but it exuded the feeling of a home. Lucy had told me that she always left the door unlocked and had instructed me where to find the dog food. I felt strange going in her house, so I stopped by the local grocery store and bought a bag of dog food.

It was getting pretty dark, and my breath flowed out in frozen mist. There were two shiny bowls on the edge of the porch as reported. I took one to a hydrant and filled it with water. I left the water barely running so the pipe wouldn't freeze. Then I filled the other with dog food. I opened the front door and put the bag of dog food just inside. Then I closed the door again.

It seemed so peaceful that my soul felt still. With my hands in my pockets, I wandered around to the back of the house, whistling for Panda. He bounded up to me, and I rubbed his spotted, furry head. I gave him a pat on the rump as he raced toward the food bowls at the front of the house.

To my right was the old board barn. I walked to it and pushed on the door. The hinges creaked as it opened a foot. I turned sideways and sidled in. There was the hay. The strings had already been cut, and a few flakes were missing. I took two of the flakes and sidled back outside with them. I closed the door and tossed the flakes onto the ground beside the barn.

I turned to head back toward the jeep. That's when I saw him. There in front of me was a white stallion with a long mane, blowing in the wind. He was about sixteen hands high and had a dish face and a plumelike tail that stood out branding him as an Arabian. But he was taller than most Arabs.

It sounds strange, but I swear that he stared me straight in the eyes. He was a good fifty yards away, and it was dark, but our eyes locked. I got the feeling that even through his haughtiness, he appreciated me being there.

He threw his head twice, stamped his feet twice, then turned and walked into the small stand of pines without any sign of haste. I was mesmerized. I don't know how long I stood there in the cold, staring after him, but it felt like hours. Slowly, I turned and walked to the front of the house.

There was Panda, calmly eating his dog food. He had been oblivious to the majestic presence of the stallion. Oh well, there's no accounting for taste.

I got in the jeep and made the loop. When I reached the highway, I turned right and headed back toward town.

Just at the edge of town was the Wheatland Inn. They serve breakfast there all day and into the night. I was starving, and I had heard many people talk about the hamburgers there. I parked the jeep and sauntered inside.

It was bright and home looking. I took off my cowboy hat—an attempt to fit in with the locals—and was led to an empty table. There were a few cowboys and a few hefty women seated around, but many of the tables were vacant. I ordered a burger and a Sprite.

A young lady with an obviously pregnant waist brought my burger and Sprite with a glass of ice. It smelled wonderful. I wolfed down the burger and drank half the Sprite then paid the ticket, leaving a nice tip.

I got in the jeep and headed home. When I got there, I found the house rather cool, almost cold. The water pipes ran freely, so they were not frozen. After watching a little TV, I went to bed.

Next morning, I entered Lucy's room with her chart, which I had already studied.

"Well, Lucy, you seem to be doing better this morning," I began.

"Well, good morning to you, hon." Lucy smiled.

"Okay, it seems that you're ready to go home today," I continued.

"That's awful nice of you, sweetie," she crooned.

"All right, you may go home after lunch. I will have a couple of prescriptions for you, and I expect you to take them," I stated. "And I would like to see you again in the office in two weeks."

"How was Panda?" she queried.

"Panda was fine. I fed and watered him, and he seemed very satisfied."

"He is a good boy," Lucy intoned.

I closed the chart as I stood up. "Once again, I will see you in two weeks."

But I didn't see her in two weeks. In fact, it was almost two months before I saw her.

Lucy was back in the office just before Thanksgiving. Her ankles looked like those of an elephant, and yellowish fluid seeped from them with any pressure.

"Have you been taking your Lasix?" I quizzed her after a quick exam.

"Usually, hon," she cooed.

I glanced at her chart. "You have gained twenty pounds, and you don't look too good."

"Well, you don't look too great either, hon," she joked.

"You haven't been taking your medicine, have you?" I chided.

"That stuff is expensive. And I have too much to do to spend all day in the pisser."

"Have you been having any chest pain?" I inquired.

"Not much," she confessed.

"Not much means you have been having some."

"Yeah, some," Lucy admitted.

"You need to be back in the hospital," I intoned blandly.

"Can't," she argued.

"Why not this time?" I countered. "Got company coming for Thanksgiving?"

"Nope, no company. I usually help cook Thanksgiving lunch at the senior center."

"Well, this time"—I sucked in my breath—"someone else will have to help."

That night on rounds, I was sure to study Lucy's chart before I entered her room.

"How are you feeling tonight?" I inquired pleasantly.

"Good, thank you. How are you?" she quizzed.

"I am fine, thanks."

I examined her and found her lungs sounded better though still wet. Her ankles were much less swollen, but she had been lying down most of the day. Then I sat down to scribble in the chart.

"I been pissing all day," she complained.

"That's the idea." I chuckled.

"Have a cup of coffee, hon. You can't be in such an all-fired hurry every day," she invited.

Usually, I don't drink caffeine after lunch because it keeps me awake, but somehow I felt the need to comply. "OK."

"I can only have one cup at night," she griped.

"Yes, I know, it is my order," I agreed as I tapped the chart. I stood. "I will be right back."

I went to the little kitchenette off the hall and poured two small Styrofoam cups full of coffee. With the chart under my arm and a cup of coffee in each hand, I returned to her room.

I gave her one cup then sat in the chair with my cup.

"The idea is you have too much fluid. So we don't want to put in more than we take out. We want to drain some," I explained.

"Sure, sure, hon." She sipped her coffee. She leaned back on the bed. "I remember a Thanksgiving when I was young—maybe about sixteen . . . It was 1935 . . ."

# CHAPTER 2

S HEEP MOUNTAIN IS about fourteen miles northwest of Wheatland. Several ridges flow down the sides of the mountain like dragon toes. On one of these ridges, about a third of the way up, Paul Johansson began digging his gold mine. He mined about twenty feet into the side of the mountain before realizing his gut feeling about gold being there was disappointing as he found only a small amount. He then turned the mine into his dwelling. With the inside shored and a room walled off, it became a house. Two years later, he built a front room, which projected out of the mountain. It is called a berm house.

Paul Johansson served with the Fourth Michigan Infantry during the American Civil War. He was wounded at the Battle of the Wilderness and survived with an empty sleeve on his left arm from the elbow down. He moved to Wyoming in 1867, seeking fame and fortune. He found neither. He began prospecting on Sheep Mountain and dug a mine about one-third of the way up. Folks in those parts always wondered how he was able to do this one-handed.

He met an Indian named Runs with Wind. They were married by a traveling Catholic priest in 1868. In 1870, his son, George Johansson, was born. The mine, which had only produced two handfuls of gold, was then turned into a one-room house. Paul often said that it didn't produce any ore anyway.

In 1888, George met an Indian girl named Bad Foot. Shortly after marrying her, the Indian died of causes unknown. He began trapping around Cottonwood Creek. His hunting ground often took him close to the road from Wheatland north. In the late fall of 1889, while running his traps on Cottonwood Creek, he encountered a wagon traveling north. It contained the Carlson family. Herbert Carlson owned a ranch on the North Platte River about thirty miles north of Wheatland. The family was on its way home from Wheatland, where they had spent two days buying and loading supplies. The wagon contained a sixteen-year-old blond-haired girl with sparkling green eyes, named Lucy Carlson. George found her breathtaking. Lucy was a little hesitant. After two months of courtship, George and Lucy were married in 1890.

Lucy and George had three children. Lucy Paulene Johansson was born in 1895. She died in 1897. Michael Johansson was born in 1896. Carl Johansson was born in 1900.

George assisted in the building of Reservoir Number 1 as well as taking care of the home and what land he had. By 1905, he was able to dig a well beside the house and have water in the house year-round to wash, clean, and cook. Ms. Lucy was elated to have water immediately available in the house instead of having to carry buckets of water over a hundred yards from the stream.

Carl Johansson grew quickly and was the spitting image of his father. He was tall, dark haired, and blue-eyed. He had a barrel chest and thick, well-muscled arms and chest. He met Erin Schmidt in 1916 and fell in love immediately. Erin's father was a cattle rancher on the Wheatland plains. They were married in 1917.

George Johansson, Carl's father, had taken some of Paul's gold, laid claim to three hundred acres of land, and bought a small herd of cattle, consisting of four heifers and one bull. With Carl's marriage, George enlisted the aid of Erin's father to increase the herd.

In 1918, Carl, along with his brother, Michael, enlisted in the army. They were sent to Europe and both fought at the Battle of Belleau Woods in France. Carl returned to Wyoming almost completely deaf and with some German shrapnel embedded in his back. Michael did not return, and his body was never found.

Carl settled in as a cattle rancher. He added several rooms to the front of the mine, which had been turned into a house. Shortly after Carl had returned to Wyoming, his father fell asleep and never woke up.

Carl did well as a cattle rancher and bought two hundred acres at the base of Sheep Mountain. His herd continued to increase. In 1922, Carl Johansson Jr. was born. In 1923, Lucy Johansson, who was named after her dead aunt, was born.

By 1930, Lucy had grown into a tall, lanky young lady. She would rise early every morning, milk their single milk cow, and ride on horseback to the town of Wheatland to school. She excelled in reading and writing but had some difficulty in math.

Then the stock market crashed in 1929. This had little effect on the Johanssons. However, the rest of the country was greatly affected.

By 1931, the drought, which affected the Midwest and created the Oklahoma dust bowl, became a concern to the citizens of Wheatland. For the next few years, Carl Sr. helped the workers of WPA reconstruct Reservoir Number 2. His wife, Erin, helped cook for these workers. Together, they saved their money and did well.

Lucy grew, and in the fall of 1935, with the permission of her parents, she decided not to return to school. She stayed home and helped Carl Jr. take care of the ranch. Carl Sr. helped build a gas station in Wheatland, and he worked there after it was built.

And thus, on November 28, 1935, Lucy and Carl Sr. were finishing up the chores as Carl Jr. checked fences. The shadows were lengthening, and a cold north wind was blowing with eight to twelve inches of snow on the ground. Lucy and her father were carrying water down the decline to the barn, where they kept the milk cow. Her father felt a tug on his arm that he was holding the large bucket of water with, and he realized that Lucy had stopped.

"Who is that?" quizzed Lucy.

Carl looked at her and followed her eyes downhill. He studied the darkening shadows. "I don't know." He squinted his eyes. "I don't see anyone."

"He went into that stand of pine," commented Lucy. "It was a man on a horse."

"Don't know who would be riding up here the day before Thanksgiving." Carl shook his head. "Must have just been the shadows."

They walked a few more yards. "No, look." Lucy pointed. "There are horse's footprints in the snow."

"Hoofprints." Carl shook his head again. "Horses leave hoofprints, not footprints."

"OK, hoofprints. But they are there in the snow."

"Come on, we need to get this water to the cow," clucked Carl.

They watered the cow and threw some hay in the pen for her. Then they walked out, carrying the empty bucket. "There he is . . . behind the barn," said Lucy under her breath. "Keep walking." Carl could barely hear her above the wind, but he understood. "Drop the bucket when I say *now*," he instructed. They walked up the hill until they were just beyond the barn. "Now!" yelled Carl.

They dropped the bucket, and in one fluid motion, Carl swung around to face the horseman. He had the .44 pistol cleared from its holster and pointed at the man. "Who are you and what are you doing here?"

The man dismounted the horse slowly. "I got no quarrel with you folks. Just looking for some place to spend the night."

"Do not move." Carl walked slowly toward the man, gun still pointed. Lucy stood transfixed as Carl advanced on the man. He stopped only three feet away. "Who are you and where do you come from?" He tilted his head. "I don't remember seeing you around here."

"I am Charles Morgan . . . Charlie. I come from Oklahoma."

Carl listened carefully. He could tell by the cracking voice that the man was young—very young. "How old are you, son?"

"Twenty, sir," answered the young man quickly.

"No, you aren't," pronounced Carl calmly.

"OK, I'm sixteen. But I have travelled all the way from Oklahoma."

"By horse?" Carl holstered the pistol.

"Well . . . ," began Charlie.

"Wait a minute," interrupted Carl. "That horse looks very familiar." He stepped closer to the horse. "That's Alex Johnson's Arabian stud."

"I rode the rails from just outside Tulsa to somewhere past Cheyenne and then took to horse," admitted Charlie.

"How much did you pay for the horse?" asked Carl with a sly smile.

"I didn't have to pay much," said Charlie, looking down and kicking at the snow.

"Well, put the horse in the barn. There is an empty stall beside the cow. Then come to the house. We will discuss it." He turned to walk back to Lucy then turned back to Charlie. "You do know they still hang horse thieves, don't you?" Not waiting for an answer, he walked to where Lucy was standing and lifted one side of the empty water bucket. "Come on, Lucy, let's get back to the house."

The house was warm from the stove, which served for cooking and warmth. The smell of beef stew permeated the small house. Carl and Lucy entered the house, and Lucy hurried to the sink and washed her hands. As she was wiping her hands, Carl Jr. entered the house.

"The fence is all good," announced Carl Jr. He went to the sink and shoved Lucy to the side with his shoulder. "Did you know there is a boy in the barn?"

"Yep," agreed Carl Sr.

Erin, Lucy's mother, was stirring the beef stew. "There is a boy in the barn?" she asked.

"Yep." Carl Sr. nodded.

"What is he doing there?"

"He is putting Alex Johnson's Arabian stud in a stall," sighed Carl Sr., leaning back.

"Well, go get him for supper, Junior," Erin demanded.

Carl Jr. looked at his father. Carl Sr. tilted his head toward the door. "Yes, ma'am," answered Carl Jr. as he walked to the door.

"What is a boy doing with Mr. Johnson's stud? And who is he? Where did he come from?" mused Erin.

"I don't know the answer to any of those questions yet. Except where he came from. He came from Oklahoma."

"Well, what is he doing here?" mused Erin.

Carl Sr. let out a deep sigh. "I don't know yet, honey. I will find out when the time comes. Let's feed him for now. I am sure he must be hungry."

Soon they were all seated around the table with large bowls of stew and a hunk of homemade bread in front of them. The table was large enough for six, but they only had four chairs, so Lucy sat on a stool. This brought her chin just to table height. Throughout the ensuing conversation, she could not take her eyes off the young blond-haired stranger. His blue eyes twinkled in the light of the kerosene lamp, which hung over the table. Occasionally, Charlie would look at her and, seeing her staring at him, would drop his eyes to the stew.

After supper, Carl Sr. rolled a cigarette and sat back in his chair. "So, son, what brings you to Wyoming all the way from Oklahoma?"

"The family farm blew away just like all the others in the dust bowl. My parents, brother, and two sisters were loading up to move to California. I decided to head for Wyoming. My mother's brother lives in a place called Laramie, so I decided to go see them." He looked around. "How far is it to Laramie?"

"Laramie is about three days' ride from here through Bosler Canyon. But that is on horseback, and you don't have a horse," Carl Sr. quipped.

"I have a horse," responded Charlie indignantly.

"You have a stolen horse. It's not yours," accused Lucy.

Carl Sr. gave her a stern look. "You stay out of this, missy." Carl turned his attention back to Charlie. "You sleep in the barn tonight. We will loan you some blankets, and you can pile hay around you. Tomorrow you can have Thanksgiving with us, then Friday, we will go together and talk to Mr. Johnson."

Charlie hung his head. "Yes, sir." He looked back up at Carl Sr. "Thank you, sir."

"Mama"—Carl Sr. looked at Erin—"get the boy some blankets, please."

"Don't worry, Papa will help you get this straightened out with Mr. Johnson," assured Lucy.

Charlie took the blankets and walked to the barn in the dark in two and a half feet of snow. It was still snowing, but he only stumbled once. He made sure the horse was comfortable in a stall and threw some hay to him.

Early the next morning, he woke just before daylight, broke the thin ice over the water trough, and washed his face. The icy water was bracing, to say the least. He then walked slowly back to the house. He was not sure anyone else was awake, so he walked around outside the house softly.

The door opened, and Carl Jr. stuck his head outside. "Come on in. Breakfast is ready."

"Thanks," announced Charlie, hurrying into the house. It was warm inside, and the entire family, except for Erin, was seated around the table. Erin was busying herself, setting plates of eggs, bacon, and toasted homemade bread in front of each. There was a plate for Charlie between the two Carls. The warmth comforted Charlie like a woman's arms. The house smelled of cooked bacon with a hint of smoke.

"After breakfast," began Carl Sr., "we will head to town and talk to Mr. Johnson."

Charlie looked up. "Now?" he quizzed with his mouth full of food. "I thought we were going tomorrow."

"We will take the truck. We can be there and back before Mother has the potatoes ready," answered Carl Sr. "The sooner this is settled, the better."

"Yes, sir," agreed Charlie, hanging his head.

Alex Johnson answered the knock at the door. "Good morning, Carl, what brings you here at this hour?" quizzed Alex.

"You have a horse missing." Carl looked him straight in the eyes. "A stallion, I believe."

"I really haven't looked today." Alex cleared his throat. "It is Thanksgiving, you know."

"I know, Alex, and I hate to bother you," replied Carl. "But I have your stallion up at my place."

"How did he get there? I just checked the fence last week. It was very sturdy," averred Alex.

"He got to my place with the help of this lad," explained Carl.

Alex Johnson looked Charlie up and down. "A horse thief? He looks kinda scrawny for a horse thief."

"I am not a horse thief," explained Charlie. "I just borrowed him."

Alex looked from Charlie to Carl and back to Charlie. "You led that stallion all the way to Carl's?"

"No, sir," said Charlie, hanging his head. "I rode him."

Alex's jaw dropped. "You rode him? You rode the stallion?"

"Yes, sir."

Alex looked at Carl. "That horse is not broken. He is just for breeding. He can't be ridden," stammered Alex.

"I saw the boy ride him. He didn't seem to have any problems," confirmed Carl.

Alex scratched at his thinning hair. "Well, I'll be."

"He will return the horse tomorrow," assured Carl. "I will follow him the whole way." Carl stared straight at Alex. "That is, if you won't charge this boy with theft."

Alex chuckled. "All right." He looked at Charlie. "What kind of work do you do?"

"I was a farmer in Oklahoma. I trained horses, tilled the soil, planted, and did most of the rest. My pa died when I was young."

"Can you train that horse to be ridden?"

"He rode the horse up to my place," asserted Carl.

"What?" exclaimed Alex.

"Yep, rode that stallion right up to my place," reaffirmed Carl.

"But that horse has never had a saddle on it," stated Alex.

"I don't think he still has. The boy rode him bareback."

"Bareback?" Alex scratched his head. "And you can do this so anyone can ride him?"

"Yes, sir. I can do it easily. He is a very smart horse. He can do anything you want," assured Charlie.

"Well, bring the horse back next week"—he looked at Carl—"if you will take responsibility of making sure it is returned."

"Of course." Carl nodded.

"See if you can get that horse to be ridden in that time. If so, you can do some work for me." Alex looked sharply at Charlie. "That is, if you want."

"Yes, sir, it will be easy. Like I said, he is a very smart horse. In three days I can have him so that anyone can ride him," assured Charlie.

On the ride home, Carl further quizzed Charlie. "How can you be sure the horse will be turned from a breeding stallion to a saddle horse? After all, he is a stallion."

"He is a stallion, but he wants to please. Just have to make him understand what you want," assured Charlie.

"Huh," grunted Carl.

They arrived at the house well before noon. Carl parked the truck, and he and Charlie trudged to the house. They opened the door and were assailed by warmth and the scent of cooking turkey, mashed potatoes, and sweet potatoes.

Charlie took off his hat. "That smells wonderful," complimented Charlie.

"Thank you." Erin blushed.

"How close are we to eating?" groused Carl Sr.

"Hours," complained Carl Jr.

"It will be ready in about an hour," corrected Erin.

"Are you hungry?" inquired Lucy shyly.

"Starved," answered Charlie, blushing.

"While we are waiting, how about a walk?" asked Lucy.

Charlie looked at Carl Sr.

"Can you two behave yourselves?" demanded Carl Sr.

"Yes, sir," replied Lucy and Charlie at the same time.

"All right, but don't take too long. It is cold out there," assented Carl Sr.

Charlie helped Lucy into her coat and shrugged on his own. They walked onto the porch and breathed the cold, clean air.

"Show me your wonderful horse," demanded Lucy.

"Well, he is not my horse . . . yet," responded Charlie. "He's in the barn." Charlie waved his arm toward the barn.

"Lead the way, my prince," twittered Lucy.

Charlie blushed again and turned toward the barn. His stride was long and swift.

"Wait up," griped Lucy. "A lady can't walk that fast."

"Sorry," responded Charlie, blushing again.

They arrived at the barn, and Charlie gallantly opened the door for her. They walked in, and Charlie led the way to the stallion's stall.

"Oh, he is so lovely," exclaimed Lucy. "What is his name?"

Charlie hadn't thought about that. He had no idea what the horse's name was. "I don't know what it was, but I call him Coeur."

"Cur? That is a funny name for a horse. That is what they call a dog of questionable parentage."

"No, Coeur. It is French for *heart*. And this fine boy is all heart," answered Charlie, shuffling his feet in the dust.

"Oh, you speak French," exclaimed Lucy, delighted.

"Just a little. My mother was French. My dad met her during the Great War," explained Charlie.

"Well, he is beautiful." Lucy beamed.

"He is magnificent," whispered Charlie.

Lucy, who had been staring at Charlie's face throughout the conversation, turned her gaze back to the horse. "Yes, he is magnificent." She turned back to Charlie. "Like you." She stood on tiptoes and kissed Charlie on the cheek. Then she giggled and ran out of the barn and back to the house.

Charlie stood there in a daze for what seemed hours, then, confused, trudged through the snow back toward the house. "What the hell got into her?" he mused aloud. Then he reached the door of the house and, after first stomping the snow from his boots, entered. The table was set elegantly. It looked and smelled wonderful.

The turkey was moist, the potatoes smooth, and the gravy blended just right with the cranberry sauce. Charlie ate so much that he was able to eat only one large slice of the pumpkin pie. Lucy stared at Charlie throughout the whole meal and only played with her food.

"Lucy, you have hardly eaten," admonished Erin.

"I'm not very hungry," Lucy replied.

"Are you sick, child?" queried Carl Sr. He turned toward Charlie. "She usually eats more than all the rest of us combined."

"Yes, sir." Charlie blushed, unable to think of anything else to say.

"Mother! Daddy!" complained Lucy.

Carl Sr. laughed.

"Don't tease the child, Carl," ordered Erin.

"Yes, Mama." Carl looked at Charlie. "She runs this house with an iron hand."

"Now you have embarrassed the whole table," accused Erin.

"He hasn't embarrassed me," mumbled Carl Jr. with his mouth full of food.

"Don't talk with your mouth full," commanded both Carl Sr. and Erin at the same time.

After the meal, the two Carls and Charlie sat in front of the fire while Erin and Lucy cleaned the table and washed the dishes.

"Well, son, what are your plans now?" quizzed Carl Sr.

"I don't exactly know, sir. Perhaps I can help do odd jobs here and there," responded Charlie.

"Well, we could put you up here for a week or so . . . until you can find a place of your own," commented Carl Sr. "Unless, of course, you are in a hurry to make your way to Laramie or parts beyond."

"No, sir. I would appreciate staying here for a little." Charlie nodded. He looked over his shoulder at Lucy. "Besides, I need to get that stallion trained and returned to Mr. Johnson."

"How much do you know about automobiles?" interrogated Carl Sr.

"A lot, sir. I kept my family's Ford going for ten years. Even got them out toward California," explained Charlie.

"Well, I know old Lester at the Grease Spot Garage. Maybe he can give you a job," mused Carl Sr. "We can go talk to him tomorrow."

Charlie was watching Lucy closely and was slow to respond to Carl.

"Charlie?"

"Yes, sir." Charlie looked at Carl. "That would be swell, sir."

"Good. Then tomorrow we will see about getting you established around here," agreed Carl Sr., sitting back.

"I hear you are good with horses," commented Carl Jr.

"I do OK," responded Charlie.

"Old man Johnson's stallion give you any problems?"

"Nope. He just needed to know what I wanted from him. He is smart and willing." Charlie smiled.

"Would I be able to ride him? I am a fair horseman."

"Not yet. He still needs to learn a few things. By Monday you could ride him," explained Charlie.

"Well, I will plan on riding him Monday." Carl Jr. smiled.

"Yep, that would be fine." Charlie grinned.

# CHAPTER 3

C HARLIE MADE A small room in the barn and slept on a bed of hay. He covered up with a quilt that Mrs. Johansson loaned him. He worked the stallion until it was gentle and willing to do anything he asked.

"You gonna have New Year's lunch with us tomorrow?" asked Carl Sr.

"Sure. You gonna have some black-eyed peas?" quizzed Charlie.

"Black-eyed peas?" puzzled Carl.

"Sure. Give you good luck all year. Gotta have some black-eyed peas," explained Charlie. "Make 1938 a good year."

"Sure. I can scare up some." Carl chuckled. "Erin will have a regular feast."

"Is Lucy going to be there?" asked Charlie shyly.

"Of course. It will be a family meal," replied Carl.

Charlie looked down and smiled, shuffling his feet.

"You warm enough in that barn?" inquired Carl.

"Yes, sir. Got a good quilt. Barn blocks the wind really good," responded Charlie.

"This spring," began Carl, "you can build a small house on some of the land I have at the bottom of the hill."

"Really?" shouted Charlie. "I mean, thank you, sir."

"Sure. Just make it a good house. Not some shotgun crap that will be an eyesore," retorted Carl.

"I gotta go take care of my horse," stated Charlie suddenly.

Carl dropped his head and gave Charlie a hard look. "Whose horse?"

"I mean, Mr. Johnson's horse," replied Charlie meekly. He turned and hurried out of the Johansson house.

The next day, Charlie woke early. The air was cold and still. He washed his face in cold water he kept in the barn for his personal hygiene. He toweled off with a rag he kept near the bucket for that purpose. He took a deep breath and used the icy water to clean under his arms. Goose bumps raised on both his arms. He put on his cleanest clothes and went outside to the side of the barn farthest from the house and relieved himself. He finished cleaning and walked through the howling wind to the main house. The wind bit through his thin clothing, but the smell of roasted turkey wafted on the same wind and enticed him on.

"Welcome, Charlie," greeted Erin.

"Good morning, Mrs. Johansson," Charlie returned. "Is Lucy awake yet?"

"Oh yes." Erin grinned. "She is still in her room, primping." Erin chuckled. "Says she needs to look special today."

"Oh," responded Charlie. He walked to the table and pulled out a chair. He sat down heavily.

"You look mighty nice today," commented Erin.

"Thank you, ma'am." Charlie nodded. He looked around the room. The place was spotless. The room was warmed by the oven in which the turkey was roasting. Also, a pot of water was boiling on the stove with chopped-up potatoes in it. Another pot bubbled with an unknown content.

"Your black-eyed peas are cooking," commented Erin, waving toward the second pot. "It took a little doing, but we got some."

"Thank you, ma'am," said Charlie.

"Actually, we had some in the cellar," admitted Erin.

Just then, Lucy entered through the interior door, which separated the kitchen from the living quarters. Her honey-colored hair hung loosely to the small of her back. The sides were pulled back and clipped in the back with a silver hair clasp. The sun shone through the kitchen window right on her face without being directly in her eyes. It highlighted her high cheekbones and gave her cheeks a ruby glow. Her sparkling blue eyes twinkled with youth and the promise of life. She looked at Charlie, and her cheeks reddened even more.

"Good morning, Mr. Morgan." Lucy curtsied.

Charlie was confused. In the two months he had known Lucy, she had never been so formal. "Good morning, Ms. Johansson."

"I am delighted you were able to join us," replied Lucy.

"Stir the potatoes," Erin ordered Lucy, barely able to contain her mirth.

Lucy walked to the pot of boiling potatoes and stirred the pot. "The potatoes are almost done," stated Lucy formally.

"The turkey is not quite done yet," commented Erin. "Turn the flame down a little."

Lucy turned the knob, which lowered the flame under the potatoes. She then twirled around, causing her blue-and-white calico dress to swirl around her spindly legs.

Carl Sr. entered the room. "Good morning, Charlie," he greeted. "Did you sleep well?"

"Yes, sir," Charlie stammered without taking his eyes off Lucy.

Carl grinned at Erin. "Good morning, darling."

"Good morning, husband. The food won't be ready for a while. Would you and Charlie like a biscuit to tide you over?" she answered.

"That would be fine," responded Carl.

"Yes, ma'am," responded Charlie, finally looking away from Lucy.

Carl and Charlie ate ravenously. They had no time to talk as they were satisfying their hunger. Finishing quickly, Carl wiped his mouth and sat back.

"So, Charlie, have you talked to Lester Martin yet?" asked Carl.

Charlie wiped his mouth as he finished chewing the last bite of biscuit. "Yes, sir. I spoke to him the other day," replied Charlie, looking at Lucy.

"I am over here, boy," scolded Carl. "What did he say?"

Charlie looked back at Carl. "I am to start work there Monday."

"Good, good. Now you work hard and don't make me sorry," lectured Carl. "You know I work there some too."

"Yes, sir," replied Charlie.

"Are you going to work at the garage?" asked Lucy.

"Of course he is. Didn't you just hear him?" scoffed Carl.

Lucy looked at Carl and screwed up her face. Then she quickly straightened up as she saw the menacing look on Carl's face. "Yes, sir." She looked back at Charlie, smiling. "I am glad you are going to be working here." She looked down and thought a minute then looked back up. "I mean work in Wheatland . . . in the area." She flushed again and turned back to the boiling potatoes. She stirred them vigorously.

"Stir the potatoes gently," chided Erin.

"Yes, ma'am," responded Lucy.

They heard stomping on the porch, and a second later, the door opened. Carl Jr. entered, brushing the snow from his coat. "Broke the ice over the water for the cows and threw them some hay." He looked at Charlie. "I broke the ice over the water tank beside the barn. You can water your horse there."

"That is Mr. Johnson's horse," snapped Lucy.

"No." Charlie smiled. Carl, Carl Jr., Erin, and Lucy stared at Charlie. "I made a deal with Mr. Johnson. He made me a good deal, and I can make payments on the horse." He beamed. "The horse will be mine by June."

"Well, good for you, son." Carl grinned, slapping Charlie on the back.

Two hours later, the five of them were seated around the table, partaking of a feast very similar to the Thanksgiving meal. After they had all eaten their fill, Lucy turned to Charlie.

"Want to go for a walk?" she asked.

"Wait a while," said Carl. "The boy needs to let his food digest. Besides, it is cold out there."

"It is all right, sir," stated Charlie, holding his hand up. "I would enjoy a brisk walk."

Lucy put on her coat and strode to the door. Charlie rose and adjusted his thin overshirt.

"Here, boy," laughed Carl. "Take my coat. You will freeze out there like that."

Charlie shrugged into Carl's jacket, which was a size too large, and opened the door for Lucy. The two marched out into the gray sky, which had, for the moment, quit spitting snow. They trudged through the snow on the ridge above the house, walking toward the tree line above the house. When they reached the first few trees, Charlie turned to Lucy.

"Are you cold, Lucy?" he asked.

"Not so much," she answered. She looked into the blue eyes and felt her soul swimming. "I mean," she stammered, "a little."

Charlie took her into his arms and wrapped her tight. He pressed his cheek against hers and felt the warmth. "I love you," he whispered into her ear.

"I love you too," she whispered back.

He pulled his face back slightly then leaned forward and kissed her deeply and long. "Marry me?" he asked softly.

"Is that a question?" she replied as softly.

"Yes."

"Then I will answer tomorrow." She laughed. "A girl has to think about things like that."

Charlie dropped his arms to his side and frowned.

"Oh, silly," she squealed, wrapping her arms about his waist. "Can't you tell when I am kidding? Of course I will marry you!"

"You will?" he said, not believing his ears.

"Yes, yes, a thousand times yes." She giggled.

In late March of 1938, Charlie and Lucy were married at the First Methodist Church and became Mr. and Mrs. Charles Morgan.

# CHAPTER 4

"CHARLIE, HAVE YOU patched Mr. Drube's inner tube yet?" inquired Lester Martin.

"Yes, sir, it is patched, aired up, and placed back on his Ford," responded Charlie.

"Good. Now you can help your father-in-law change the oil in the Packard," said Lester.

"OK. That won't take long," acknowledged Charlie.

In less than an hour, Charlie and Carl Sr. had the oil changed. The two then went to the bench in front of the garage. Carl Sr. lit up a cigar and handed another to Charlie.

"Here, enjoy."

"Thanks," replied Charlie, taking the cigar.

Carl blew out a large puff of bluish smoke. "You have been here for four years now—well, almost four years." He took another puff of the cigar. "You have bought some land, married my daughter, and settled here. Now what?"

Charlie took a puff off his cigar. "Well, I finally paid off Mr. Johnson, and Coeur is mine now." He took another puff. "Now it is time to start a family."

Carl Sr. leaned back and looked up at the June clouds. "You and Lucy have been married for, what is it, two years now?"

"Three years," corrected Charlie.

"Three years." Carl took another puff. "Yep, it is time."

"If it is a boy, what are you going to name him?" questioned Carl.

"Well, not Carl, that's for sure," grunted Charlie.

Carl chuckled. "No. That one is taken."

"Probably Michael. After the archangel," mused Charlie.

"It is a good name," agreed Carl. "Come on, it's quitting time. I will give you a ride home."

"Thanks."

Still puffing on the cigars, the two pulled down the garage doors and locked them. They then climbed into Carl's old truck and headed west.

After supper, as Lucy was putting the dishes in the sink filled with water warmed on the stove, Charlie said, "Have you given any thought to having a baby?"

"We have discussed this already. When it happens, it happens. It is not something you and I plan. It is a gift from God." She dropped her head. "It will just . . . happen."

Charlie rose and walked to her. He took her shoulders and turned her around so that she faced him. He put his arms around her and pulled her close. He could feel her breasts pressing against his chest. He pressed his crotch against hers.

"It will not just happen. We have to give it a little help." He kissed her forehead. "And have a little fun at the same time." Lucy melted into his arms.

"But I have to wash the supper dishes," Lucy remonstrated.

"Let the dishes wait," whispered Charlie, nuzzling her ear.

"It's too hot. I am melting," protested Lucy softly, not convincingly.

"It is June," whispered Charlie softly.

"We can't."

"Yes, we can. Come with me," cooed Charlie, taking her by the hand and leading her gently to the bedroom.

Once in the darkening bedroom, he gathered her in his arms again and slowly, deeply kissed her. He continued gentle contact of his lips on hers as he unbuttoned her housedress. He hungrily kissed her harder as he slipped the straps of her dress off her shoulders. The dress fell silently to the floor. He pulled his head back with half-closed eyes. Dreamily, he drank in the view of her supple, rounded, naked body. He guided lightly and pushed her backward to the bed. She sat down on the bed, breaking the embrace.

Charlie took a half step backward and jerked the suspenders from his shoulders. He hastily pulled his shirt over his head. He unbuttoned his pants with shaking hands. He vigorously yanked his feet from the pants legs. He fell as a mighty oak onto the bed, and they both giggled.

They made love with purposeful, almost violent, passion.

Charlie woke early the next morning and, still naked, walked to the kitchen sink and finished washing the dishes. He then got dressed, brushed his teeth, wetted and combed his hair, and headed to work at the garage.

"Think you can get this Studebaker sedan running again?" questioned Lester rhetorically as soon as he saw Charlie. He knew Charlie could get any machine running as long as most of the parts were there.

"What's wrong with it, sir?" questioned Charlie.

"It runs good for a while, then begins 'bumping,' then stops altogether."

"Bumps?" inquired Charlie.

"You know." Lester put his hands out as holding on to a steering wheel and shook them. "Bumps."

"Yeah, I know." Charlie went into the garage and pulled on his coveralls. He walked over to the light blue Studebaker. He lifted the hood then leaned over the engine. He reached into his coverall pocket and pulled out a crescent wrench.

"What you doin'?" came an inquiry from behind Charlie.

Charlie stood up and turned around. There was Carl Sr. "Working on getting this carburetor off." He grinned. "The car goes 'bump.'"

"Goes bump, huh," grunted Carl.

"Yep." Charlie turned back to the engine. "It must be the carburetor or the . . . wait a minute." He thrust his hand into the very maw of the engine. "Get in and turn her over." He threw some twigs and dirt onto the ground as Carl turned the key. The engine roared to life. Charlie stood straight and looked at Carl. He drew his finger across his throat, and Carl turned the engine off.

"Rat's nest in the air intake," stated Charlie simply.

"Humph," replied Carl.

"Still ought to remove the air filter and carburetor and clean them out," announced Charlie.

"Go ahead, kid." Carl grinned, getting out of the car.

As he worked, Charlie asked, "How is Carl Jr. doing? I haven't seen him in a couple of weeks."

"Depends on how you look at it," griped Carl Sr., with a toothpick hanging out of his mouth. "He is working up on the Two Bar Ranch." He shook his head. "I am worried about him."

Charlie looked at him. "Why?"

"The boy has no ambition. All he wants to do is ride around, checking fence and chasing girls."

Charlie chuckled. "Nothing wrong with that."

"Yes, there is," Carl complained. "He should be looking for something he can do for a living. Something permanent."

"Maybe that is what he wants, to be a permanent cowboy," responded Charlie.

"Maybe. But that ain't no life. He needs to settle down and get a real job," pronounced Carl.

"A real job like I got?" questioned Charlie.

"You have a real job. You got two," announced Carl.

"A mechanic?" retorted Charlie.

"And a horse trainer," added Carl.

"Well, mechanic is a real job. Not doing so well as a trainer," grumbled Charlie as he scraped grunge from the carburetor.

"What's the matter?" interrogated Carl.

"Everybody wants to train their own horse."

"Yeah, but they ain't nearly as good as you," complimented Carl.

"I do have an occasional problem horse that needs some extra attention," agreed Charlie. He looked up from the carburetor. "Get me a bowl of gasoline, will you, Dad?"

Carl Sr. grinned a large, toothy grin. "Sure." In moments he had returned with a small bowl of gasoline. "Do you realize that that is the first time you have called me Dad?" quizzed Carl.

"Huh?" snorted Charlie without looking up.

"I have been your father-in-law for three years, and this is the first time you have called me Dad." Carl smiled, handing him the bowl.

Charlie put the pieces of the carburetor in the bowl. "I'll bet I have called you Dad lots of times. You just may not have heard me."

"I may not have been there." Carl chuckled.

Charlie stood, placed his hands on his lower back, and pushed. "There. Let those parts soak for a while and then put it back together."

"Kinda hot for July, don't you think?" commented Carl.

Charlie glanced at him. "July is always hot."

"Not this hot." Carl sat in a wooden chair. "I remember it snowing in July."

"When?" quizzed Charlie.

"Several years back," replied Carl.

Lester walked into the shop. "What are you two doing sitting around?"

"Waiting on the next customer." Carl beamed.

"I was not sitting around, sir. I am about to put this carburetor back together," explained Charlie.

Lester glanced into the bowl. "Is that Mrs. Carson's Studebaker?"

"Yes, sir. I will have it running like new in an hour," assured Charlie.

A double ring sounded over a speaker in the shop. "OK, Carl, there is a customer. Get off your butt and make me some money so I can give you some money," ordered Lester.

Lester wandered back to his office as Carl strode out to take care of the customer—fill the tank, check the oil and water, and wash the windshield.

By the time Carl returned, Charlie had removed and cleaned the air filter.

"So how is my daughter doing? We don't see enough of her," remarked Carl.

"She is fine," rejoined Charlie. "She has been rather busy decorating the house and taking care of her garden."

The bell rang again. "Lester is going to have a good day today," commented Carl as he went out to the pumps.

"Good morning, Mr. Gilchrest," greeted Carl as he approached the lowered car window on the driver's side.

"Good morning, Carl," returned Mr. Gilchrest.

"Fill her up?" inquired Carl.

"Yes, thank you." Mr. Gilchrest wiped his sweat-covered forehead.

"How is Carl Jr. doing?" commented Mr. Gilchrest.

"He is doing fine, sir. Just needs to find his calling in life. Perhaps you have a place in your firm for him. He is a smart boy," remarked Carl.

"I am sure he is. However, I don't have any openings right now." Mr. Gilchrest nodded.

"That will be fifty cents, sir," said Carl when he had finished filling the tank and checking the car.

Mr. Gilchrest opened his wallet and removed a five. Handing it to Carl, he commented, "Do you and the missus have any plans for the Fourth?"

Carl took the bill. "No, sir. I think we will have Charlie and Lucy over and cook some steaks and do nothing." Carl straightened up. "I will be back in a minute with your change, sir."

Carl went into the office and rang up fifty cents on the cash register. He put the five in and took out four dollars and fifty cents. He returned to Mr. Gilchrest's car. "Here is your change, sir."

Mr. Gilchrest took the money and handed the fifty cents back to Carl. "There you are, Carl. Nice to see you," stated Mr. Gilchrest as he started the engine.

"Thank you, sir," acknowledged Carl as Mr. Gilchrest's car began rolling forward.

Carl walked back into the garage. Charlie was sitting in the Studebaker.

"Listen to this," Charlie commanded. He leaned forward slightly and turned the key. The engine roared into life with a purring growl. He let it run for several seconds with a Cheshire cat grin. He turned the engine off and got out. "Good as new!"

"It certainly sounds good," agreed Carl. "Say, what are you and Lucy doing on the Fourth?"

"The Fourth? Two days from now?" inquired Charlie. He thought a moment then replied, "Nothing I know of."

"How about you two come up and have dinner with us? Erin would love to visit with Lucy, and maybe you can talk some sense into Carl Jr."

"OK. I guess." He paused. "Why not?"

"Good. We'll expect you and Lucy around one," invited Carl.

"Should we bring anything?"

Carl chuckled, "You never had to bring anything before." Charlie looked hurt. Carl grinned wider. "No problem. You don't need to bring anything—just yourself and Lucy."

"What are you going to wear?" inquired Lucy.

"Jeans and this shirt," replied Charlie, holding up a short-sleeved white cotton shirt.

"No, that looks too much like your mechanic shirt. Here, wear this," commanded Lucy, holding up a yellow one.

"Yes, ma'am," chortled Charlie. "Your wish is my command."

Lucy tossed the shirt at him. "You are incorrigible."

"Wow, what a big word."

"You know what it means." Lucy blushed. "You can read too."

"Your dad said we did not need to bring anything," pointed out Charlie.

"I know what he said," Lucy retorted. "But I made some salad, and I intend to take it."

"OK, let's go. Mom and Dad will be waiting," commented Charlie.

They arrived just after noon at Carl's. Erin was bustling about the kitchen as Charlie knocked on the door.

"Come in," yelled Carl Sr.

Charlie opened the door and ushered Lucy in.

"Hello, folks," greeted Charlie.

"Well, hello, Charlie," saluted Erin. She gazed past him to Lucy. "And don't you look lovely." She took a step back. "What's going on? Something is different about you."

Lucy blushed and straightened her blouse. "I am the same old Lucy except I'm two weeks older than the last time you saw me."

Erin stepped back. "No, something is different. There is a glow in your cheeks."

"It is a hundred degrees. Of course there is a glow in my cheeks. It is called heatstroke," chided Lucy.

"Whatever, darling. Can you pour the tea and place the glasses on the table?" requested Erin.

"Certainly, Mama," acquiesced Lucy as she poured the tea.

"Help yourselves to some eggs and sausage. There is plenty," invited Carl Sr. as Charlie sat down at the table.

"Thank you, sir," said Charlie as he reached for the plate of eggs. "Where is Carl Jr.?"

"Oh, he's out, working with his horse. He will be here in a short time," replied Carl Sr.

"Isn't it a little hot?" questioned Charlie.

"That is how I'm sure he will be here in a short time." As Carl Sr. finished his sentence, Carl Jr. entered the door. "I told you," commented Carl Sr. as he waved his hand toward the door. "Perhaps you can have a talk with the bum."

"I am not a bum," exclaimed Carl Jr. "And it is hot out there."

"It is July," stated Carl Sr. flatly.

"Oh, Daddy, don't go on so," scolded Lucy. "Junior is living his life the way he wants."

"Yes," agreed Erin, "let the boy alone. It is a day of celebration."

Carl Sr. just grunted.

Erin brought the toast to the table, and Lucy set the platter of butter in the center of the table. The five sat down at the table and ate. There was not much talk at the table—not because there was nothing to say but because eating was rapid and their mouths were always full.

After brunch, the two Carls and Charlie retired to the front porch while Erin and Lucy cleared the table and washed dishes.

Flies buzzed, and Carl Jr. shooed a yellow jacket from his bare arm. They sat in lawn chairs, and each opened a beer, passing the bottle opener around to puncture the can tops. The smell of honeysuckle, which grew beside the porch, permeated the air.

Carl Sr. lit a cigarette and puffed out some smoke. He took a sip of beer and leaned back. "So, Junior, how are things at the Two Bar?"

"Good. The yearlings are growing good, and we should have a good year at the sale this fall," returned Carl Jr.

"We?" inquired Carl Sr. "What is this 'we'? You just work there."

"I know. But I am responsible for them, so I feel like they are mine. And the more money the Two Bar makes on them, the more money I will get," rejoined Carl Jr.

"Humph" was Carl Sr.'s only response.

Charlie squirmed in his chair, responding to the uncomfortable situation. "I brought some firecrackers to fire for the Fourth."

Carl Sr. looked around the yard. "It's a little dry."

"We will keep an eye on it. Have some water ready," assured Charlie.

"Yeah, Dad, let's just have fun," cajoled Carl Jr.

"Anyway, wait until it gets darker," muttered Carl Sr.

Erin and Lucy entered the porch, wiping sweat from their faces.

"What are you two talking about?" quizzed Erin.

"Just things," replied Carl Sr.

"Well"—Erin looked at Lucy—"I think Lucy has something to report."

The three men turned in their chairs to look at the women.

"Go ahead, tell us," encouraged Carl Sr.

Lucy shuffled on the oak wood porch. "It isn't much."

"What is it?" encouraged Charlie.

"Just that I am going to have a baby." She looked shyly at Charlie. "We are going to have a baby."

Charlie's mouth dropped open. Carl Jr. grinned and looked at his dirty boots. Carl Sr. leaned forward, dropped his cigarette, and stomped it out.

"Well, that is wonderful!" exclaimed Carl Sr. boisterously.

"When?" inquired Carl Jr.

Charlie sat there frozen.

"Well, the best I can figure, he will arrive in December," replied Lucy.

"That is great," exclaimed Carl Sr., moving quickly to his daughter and gently embracing her.

"Yeah, that is great," agreed Carl Jr.

Charlie sat there, staring at Lucy.

# CHAPTER 5

"A LITTLE COLD to be working horses this morning, isn't it?" questioned Lucy.

"Horses gotta be worked, and I have the day off," replied Charlie.

Charlie sat at the table and watched the snow falling heavily outside the window. The snow gave the rolling hills a cold, clean appearance.

"It's kinda cold for December, isn't it?" observed Lucy.

"It is always cold up here in December." Charlie chuckled. He looked over at her and smiled. He reached out for her and pulled her close to him. Her pregnant belly forced her to lean over and forward to kiss him. "Now, what is on your mind? I know it isn't the weather."

"Mom and Dad want us to go to their house for lunch tomorrow," Lucy confided.

"Well," began Charlie, "I am laid off for now at the garage. I have to work two horses today and tomorrow. But we should be able to leave for their house around ten." He looked at her. "Will that be early enough?"

"That will be fine." Lucy laughed.

Charlie finished his coffee and shrugged into his wool-lined jacket. He strode out the door and across the drive to the holding pen. There were two horses milling around nervously in the square pen. Charlie entered the pen, cooing softly all the time. All his movements were slow and deliberate. No wasted energy and no sudden motion.

"Come here, sweet Storm," he almost whispered at the white mare. He slowly walked up to her, barely lifting his feet but not shuffling either. He sidled up to her head and slowly stroked her forehead. Slowly, he moved his hand to her neck without ever losing contact with her thick coat. He lightly snaked his arm over her neck and moved his other hand up to her muzzle. He stroked her face close to her mouth for several seconds. Slowly, he removed his hand from her muzzle and reached into his back pocket where he had part of the lead rope stuffed—the rest trailed out of his pocket. He snaked the lead rope over her neck and reached under her neck to grab at the end of the rope. He led her slowly over to the side of the pen where the halter was hanging. He lightly haltered her and attached the lead rope, which he had used to lead her, to the halter.

He led her from the square pen to the round pen, which stood twenty yards away, talking softly, lovingly, all the time.

He walked into the round pen with her and closed the gate. He removed the lead rope and walked to the center of the pen. The mare watched him closely without moving. She lowered her head and snorted softly while watching Charlie move all the time.

Charlie reached the center of the round pen and turned back to the mare. "You know what you need to do, darling. This isn't the first time we have been here." He clucked loudly at her, and she began to trot around the perimeter of the pen. He watched her trot for four turns then stepped quickly toward her front. She pivoted toward him and began trotting the other direction.

"Good, girl. You are learning well." Charlie was in the moment and oblivious to the cold. Charlie turned twice more, then stood straight, held up his hand, and said "Whoa" loudly. The mare stopped cold and turned to face him. "Good girl," commended Charlie loudly. He dropped his hand, and the two stared at each other. The mare held her head high as she stared at Charlie. Charlie raised his right hand, palm up, and waved his fingers back toward himself. He didn't say a word. The horse watched him closely for a long second then began walking toward him. She lowered her head and licked her lips. She sidled up until her head was touching his chest. He rubbed her long mane and whispered soft encouragement to her.

Storm was white, mostly. She had several small dark spots flecking her shoulders. Her head was the typical Arabian small nose, which gave it a dish-shaped appearance. Her long forelock hung between her ears and swept across her eyes. Her dark eyes were soft, gentle, and intelligent.

Charlie looped the lead rope back around her neck. He held her in place as he slipped a bit between her teeth. She started to raise her head, and Charlie, while holding the bit in place, pushed her head back down. He seated the bit then slowly slipped the headstall past her ears. He reached under her neck and flipped the rein across her neck. She lifted her head only slightly, startled but not frightened.

Charlie moved to stand, facing her left side, continually talking softly to her. He bent his legs slightly and leaped up. At the height of his leap, he bent double so that he was lying across her back. His legs hung off her left side, and his head hung down her right side. Storm shuffled one and a half steps forward then stopped.

He cooed to her softly in nonsense verbosity. He slowly slid his right leg up and over her flank and onto her hip. Continuing to orate to her, he slipped his leg across her and sat up. Storm took one nervous step forward.

"Sweet girl," he whispered. "You are learning well." He sat up straight. "Now let's move forward easily." He kicked her softly. She moved forward hesitantly. He felt her begin to tense against his thighs. He sat down, relaxing. He was prepared for the rush and buck but did not expect it of her. She took two more steps, and he felt her begin to relax. She walked two more steps then began to trot. He felt her muscles ripple with the movement. He rode her for thirty minutes, turning her around several times and bringing her to a halt several times. Then he dismounted and rubbed her head between the eyes. He rubbed her neck as he led her back to the pen.

Then he caught the other Arab and haltered him. It was a three-year-old black gelding with a white blaze. He led him to the round pen and began to work him. He was not as far along as Storm was and needed more groundwork. He pushed him around the pen with a long lead of lunge line on the halter. He turned him several times and worked on "Halt." He would get the gelding trotting in one direction then walk quickly in front of the horse, holding up his hand and saying "Whoa." He did this several times until all he had to do was say "Whoa," and the horse would stop. He led the black gelding to the round pen and released him.

Charlie walked back to the house, stomping his feet to get the feeling to return. He stamped his feet again on the porch to remove most of the snow. He entered the house to see Lucy sitting at the kitchen table, leaning back, legs spread.

"Charlie, I think the time is close," she stated.

Charlie stopped short. "What do you mean?"

"I mean, get me to the hospital," she commanded.

"Wait here," he responded as he turned back to the door and rapidly exited. He ran through the snow to the truck and started it up. He opened the door and let off the clutch. The truck lurched forward an inch and stopped. "Damn," he cursed as he pushed the clutch back in and restarted the truck. He put it in neutral and engaged the parking brake. Then he got out and ran into the house.

He helped Lucy into the truck and jumped into the driver's seat. He headed the truck toward town, and when he hit the first bump, Lucy started screaming. She would scream for one to two minutes then sweat and grunt for five minutes. Soon, the truck bounded into town and slid through the snow-covered streets to the hospital. He brought the truck to a jolting halt and, even before the engine stopped, jumped out and ran into the hospital.

"My wife is in labor!" he shouted at the nurse sitting at the desk.

"Where is she, sir?" quizzed the nurse.

"What?" Charlie blinked, stunned. "Out in the truck."

"Don't you think we should bring her in?" inquired the nurse.

"She's out in the truck," shouted Charlie, pointing out the door.

The nurse got up and walked quickly to a wheelchair. "Let's go get her."

"Yes, come on," grunted Charlie, running to hold open the door.

The nurse got Lucy into the chair and rolled her quickly into the hospital. Even in the blown snow, Lucy was soaked with sweat.

Lucy was wheeled into the OB ward. After giving the nurse her information, Charlie sat in the waiting room, listening to the radio, which blared on the overhead speakers. He was hungry and stood to go to the nurse to ask the way to the cafeteria. Just then, the radio blared.

"This is an emergency announcement" came the disembodied voice of the announcer. "As previously announced, the American Pacific Fleet in Pearl Harbor, Hawaii, has been attacked. Preliminary reports say that the Japanese have attacked from the air and sunk most of the fleet. We will give more reports as they are available." The sounds of the Glenn Miller Band then filled the room.

The message just went in one of Charlie's ears and out the other. He had other things on his mind at the time. He walked to the nurse sitting behind a desk.

"Where is the cafeteria?" he questioned.

She looked up at him with tears rolling down her cheeks. "What?"

"Where is the cafeteria?" he repeated.

"No cafeteria," she replied. "I can get you a sandwich."

"And some milk?"

"And some water," she replied.

She scurried off to another room.

The door to the area where they had taken Lucy opened, and the doctor entered with white scrubs, a white cap, and a white mask hanging from his throat.

"Mr. Morgan?" questioned the doctor.

"Yes, sir," replied Charlie softly. He had the feeling he should talk quietly in the hospital.

"Your wife gave birth to a healthy baby girl at 2:09 PM. She and the baby are doing well," announced the doctor with a tired voice.

"How is she . . . are they?" asked Charlie.

The doctor gave a half smile. "They are fine. Wait here for a while, and then you can go in and see them."

"Here is your sandwich, sir," intoned the nurse from behind him.

Charlie turned around. "Thank you," he uttered. He took the thick white plate with the heavy bread and dark meat spilling from the sides. There was a pickle on the side. With his other hand, he took the glass of water. He then turned back to the doctor. "Thank you."

"You are welcome," returned the doctor. He seemed somewhat preoccupied. He turned and stomped down the hall.

"What is bothering him?" asked Charlie.

"His son is in the navy and stationed on a destroyer in the Pacific," she responded.

"Oh," grunted a confused Charlie. He walked to a wooden chair and sat down, balancing the plate on his lap.

The next morning, Monday, Charlie used the hospital phone to call the service station and let Lester Martin know he was not going in today. He walked down Ninth Street to the diner and ordered breakfast. As he ate, he read the *Cheyenne Tribune* newspaper that someone had left on the table. He gulped as he read the report of the attack on Pearl Harbor. He finished his breakfast, set his jaw, and walked back to the hospital.

He entered Lucy's room just as the nurse brought their daughter for her morning feeding. Charlie blushed as Lucy pulled her right breast from her gown and began feeding the baby.

Lucy looked at Charlie. "We need to give her a name. We never really talked about it, you know."

"Yeah," said Charlie, shuffling his feet.

"What about Erin?" questioned Lucy.

Charlie thought a moment. "What about Pearl?"

"Why Pearl?" responded Lucy.

"The Japanese attacked Pearl Harbor yesterday. We are now at war," answered Charlie.

"What about Erin Pearl Morgan?" bartered Lucy.

"OK. That sounds good."

"Erin Pearl Morgan," articulated Lucy, rolling the syllables in her mouth. "Erin Pearl Morgan it is then."

"Lucy," stuttered Charlie, "I gotta go sign up for the army."

"Why!" demanded Lucy.

"We are at war now. I gotta do my part," replied Charlie. "I will make sure you and Pearl are taken care of while I am gone."

"We will call her Pearl," Lucy answered. She looked at him with tears in her eyes. "I guess you have to go." She ran her hand across his cheek. "If you feel you must, then you must."

Charlie spent the rest of the day taking care of the horses, talking with Carl Sr. and his wife, Erin, and setting things in order. He ended up talking with Mr. Martin. Lester Martin told him he would have a job when he came back. By 6:00 PM, Charlie was back at the hospital.

"I been thinking, Charlie. Are you sure you gotta go?" vented Lucy.

"I am sure. I can't ask anyone else to do my part," responded Charlie.

"What about the baby?"

"Your mom and dad said they would help with the baby, and I will be sending you my army pay," encouraged Charlie.

"I love you, darling." Lucy beamed a sad smile.

"I love you too," sighed Charlie. "And I love Pearl. And because of that, I have to go."

"I know," acquiesced Lucy.

The next day, Carl Sr. took him to Cheyenne to the army enlistment depot. Charlie signed the papers, raised his hand, and was sworn into the army. He was given a voucher for a hotel room and a ride to the hotel.

Early the next morning, Wednesday, December 10, 1941, Charlie walked to the enlistment depot and met with the doctor. He passed the physical handily and was told to wait at the train station. He walked outside into the cold December sun. He walked the half mile to the train station, flapping his arms all the way to keep warm.

# CHAPTER 6

"GOOD MORNING, MS. Lucy," welcomed Lester Martin. "I see you are driving Charlie's old truck these days."

"Yes, sir," replied Lucy, pushing a recalcitrant lock of strawberry-blond hair from her forehead.

"What can I do for you today?"

"Fill her up, please, sir."

"Sure is hot for July," commented Lester as he washed the windshield.

"Sure is," agreed Lucy.

"Have you heard anything from Charlie?" inquired Lester.

"Last I heard, he had joined some new kind of unit and was training in Ireland," reported Lucy. "They call themselves rangers."

"Rangers, hunh?" grunted Lester as he gave a last swipe to the windshield with the rag he always had hanging out his front pocket. "Sure do miss the boy. The best mechanic I ever had." He walked back to the gas tank and finished filling the tank. He returned to Lucy's window. "That will be thirty cents."

Lucy handed him the change as she wiped the sweat from her eyes with her sleeve.

"That your little girl?" Lester did not wait for an answer. "She sure is growing." He clucked and shook his head. "How old is she now?"

"Yes, that is Pearl," replied Lucy. "She is eight months now."

"She sure is a good baby. Hasn't made a peep," complimented Lester. He looked closer at Pearl. "Well, I guess they are all quiet when they are asleep."

"Yes, sir," answered Lucy. "But she is always pleasant. Doesn't give me a bit of trouble."

"Well, you take care, Ms. Lucy."

"Yes, sir, thank you." Lucy nodded as she started the engine.

She put the truck in first and began rolling out onto Ninth Street. She shifted gears less than expertly but adequately and bounced down six blocks. Then she pulled over and parked in front of the library.

Lucy gathered Pearl up in her left arm and books to be returned in her right hand. She slowly exited the truck and kicked backward, closing the door. She entered the library with Pearl still asleep.

"Good morning, Ms. Morgan," welcomed the librarian, Alice Walker. Alice was two years younger than Lucy. She was tall at five feet nine inches and slight of build. Her red hair was curly and unruly; however, she attempted control by pulling it back into a ponytail. Her cheeks were always bright red as if she were permanently blushing. Her nose was flecked with freckles.

"Good morning, Alice," acknowledged Lucy. "I would like to return these books." She laid two books on the counter.

"Are you looking for another Zane Grey novel?" inquired Alice.

"Why, yes, I am," responded Lucy. "I know where they are," assured Lucy as Alice started to rise from her stool.

Lucy walked to the shelves, which held Western novels with sleeping Pearl cradled on her hip. She perused the titles of the cloth hardbound novels of Zane Grey. She found one she had never read and slid it from the shelf. She then went to a table near the newspaper section and laid the book on the table. She carried Pearl over to the newspaper rack and carefully took the Cheyenne paper. She carried it to the table where she had left her book. She sat and placed Pearl in her lap. Quickly, she looked through the paper, looking for any war news.

There were some reports from the Pacific, but she saw nothing of interest that concerned the European theatre.

Repositioning Pearl on her hip, she retraced her steps back to the front desk.

"Alice, I would like to check this one out, please," she stated softly.

"Certainly, Ms. Morgan."

Lucy frowned. "And call me Lucy."

Alice stamped the book. "Here you are, Lucy."

"Thank you," acknowledged Lucy.

"Have you heard from Mr. Morgan?" quizzed Alice.

"I received a letter two days ago," affirmed Lucy. "He is still in training in Scotland."

"Well, I hope he is OK."

Pearl squirmed and yawned as Lucy left the library. Lucy started the truck, and Pearl became fully awake. She yawned once again and blinked her eyes as she looked around.

Lucy drove a short distance to the grocery store. She lifted Pearl again and walked into the store. She got milk, some cornstarch, and some flour.

Getting back into the truck and settling Pearl in, she started the truck. Then, as Lucy started down Ninth Street, Pearl began to scream. For the rest of the drive home, Pearl continued to scream, the bellows interrupted only by an occasional pause to catch her breath.

Lucy turned into the driveway and rattled up to the front of the house. She brought the truck to a halt and let out a huge sigh as she leaned her head on the steering wheel. She carried Pearl into the house and placed her into her crib. She then went back to the truck and got her book and one bag of groceries.

She returned to the house and set about warming a small pot of water over the stove while Pearl continued to scream.

*Why can't they think of a way to heat water quickly?* Lucy thought as she poured milk into one of Pearl's bottles. She poured it half-full then added water to make it half milk, half water. *Why can't they think of a way to make kid's milk easier to fix?* She rapidly checked the heat of the water with her finger. Warm but not warm enough.

*Why can't they think of a way to shut kids up?* Lucy wondered.

Finally, the water was warm enough to put the bottle in. Pearl's cries lessened in intensity. Lucy sat down in the wooden chair with woven cane seat. Her shoulders slouched in exhaustion. She leaned her head back and closed her eyes.

Pearl's cries rose to a crescendo again.

"What do you want?" screamed Lucy, bounding to her feet. "The milk is not ready! Can't you wait just a minute?"

Lucy jerked the bottle from the near-boiling water. She squirted some of the milk onto her inner wrist. It was cool, but almost skin temperature. "That is just good enough for you, you brat!" she shrieked. She stomped to the crib and thrust the bottle into Pearl's mouth. "There!"

Pearl grabbed the sides of the bottle with her little hands and sucked hungrily. The crying and screaming stopped.

Lucy slumped heavily back into the chair. "Why can't they think of a way to heat water quickly?" she griped loudly. She leaned forward, placing her elbows on her spread legs, her head hung down. "I have to heat water on the stove to bathe, to heat her bottle, and to cook. Why can't they think of a way to heat water?" She shook her head slowly. "And where is Charlie?"

Pearl finished her bottle and went straight to sleep.

# CHAPTER 7

"GIVE THAT MAN back his pack, Private Morgan. Every man carries his own weight!" shouted the sergeant, striding rapidly to the side of Charlie.

Charlie gave the heavy pack back to Elrod Hasting, who was leaning far forward and breathing heavily. Elrod's pace slowed, and Charlie turned as he continued the march to watch Elrod fall farther back.

"Eyes front," snapped Felix "the Cat" Emerson. "Look to yourself. Make sure *you* complete the mission."

Felix was six feet two inches tall and spindly to the point of being cachectic. He was Charlie's tentmate and best friend. Felix was from Chicago and had been a taxi driver before joining the army. He appeared frail but was very strong. He had an inner toughness that was unparalleled.

They had marched at double time for five miles with a full pack and now had slowed down to route march. There were British commando sergeants wandering up and down the line, cajoling the men to "dress up the line" or "straighten that uniform."

"If that bloke tells me to button up my tunic again," grumbled Felix, "I am going to—"

"You are going to what?" questioned Charlie.

"Well, I am going to do something bad," returned Felix.

"No, seriously what are you going to do?" Charlie knew that people in Chicago settled things differently than the rest of the United States did. He remembered reading the papers about the St. Valentine's Day Massacre and the gunning down of John Dillinger. He knew Felix had been a taxi driver in Chicago, so he *must* know some lethal methods of revenge. Maybe Machine Gun Kelly had ridden in his cab at one time. Maybe Felix would use some torture to make them talk.

"I'll just get him. You'll see" was all Felix related.

They marched until around one o'clock then stopped for lunch. The British sergeant returned and spat out the order that they had ten minutes for lunch, so they had better eat fast. Charlie opened his C ration with his P-38 can opener. He wolfed down the cold hash as quickly as possible. He finished in six minutes, which was not good because eating such food so fast made his stomach cramp for two or three minutes.

Then they were on the march again. They continued until dark, around 6:00 PM. The order came down to dig slit trenches and to prepare to spend the night. Charlie drew the first watch, which lasted until around midnight. The night was cold, and Charlie had no problem staying awake as he was shivering with the cold.

At midnight, Mark White showed up at the tree, which Charlie had picked as his outpost point.

"I am here to relieve you," said Mark in a very loud whisper.

Charlie gave him a deep frown, which lost some of its authority in the dark. "Not so loud," commanded Charlie.

"OK," conceded Mark.

Charlie went back to the slit trench he had hastily dug before going on guard duty. He slept heartily until he was awakened at 0500. He wiped the sleep from his eyes as he adjusted the fifty-pound pack on his back.

The march back began easily. Most of it was downhill, which helped the stress. They were about three miles from the camp when Charlie heard bullets whine above his head. The bullets kicked out mud from the rise of land to his left. He was lying prone in the brush beside the road, readjusting his helmet before he even was aware that it was machine-gun fire.

"What the hell is going on?" demanded Mark. "Is that live ammunition?"

"Of course," explained Charlie. "Have you never been fired on before?"

"Not by my own men," retorted Mark. "In fact, I have never been fired at."

"Get used to it," commented Charlie. "These Brit commandos demand we train under actual conditions."

"Don't they know someone could get hurt?" questioned Mark.

"Of course they do," shouted Felix, who was lying prone next to Charlie. "In fact, they are trying their hardest. Your job is to *not* get hurt."

Mark crawled through the low brush to lie close to where Charlie and Felix were.

"Bet a five spot I can drop one," boasted Mark.

"Gotta see 'em first," observed Charlie.

Mark brought his Garand up slowly along the ground to seat it against his shoulder. He aimed up toward the hills, to the left of the men's original line of march. He fired a shot then put the rifle against the ground and looked over it.

"Bet I gave them a scare. Yes, sir, bet I did," gloated Mark.

"Yeah," drawled Felix. "But they is firing from the other direction."

"What?" questioned Mark, looking blank.

Charlie grinned.

"On your feet, you heathen Yanks!" yelled Sergeant Conners.

The men arose almost as one. They formed two lines and returned to the march back to camp.

That next day, the men of companies A and B were loaded on trucks and taken from Achnacarry, Scotland, to Roshven, Scotland. Charlie was billeted with a family in the town, who were in their sixties. They were very kind and understanding. Charlie could come and go without any questions. As they never locked the door, he did not need a key.

The day was spent billeting the men and making arrangements, so there was no training.

That night, Charlie met Felix in the lane, and the two friends meandered to the local pub. As they entered the pub, they spied Mark at a table, regaling two young ladies with lavish stories of his exploits. One was a buxom brunette, and the other was a slightly older bleached blonde.

Charlie and Felix looked at each other and nodded. They wandered to the bar, and each ordered a pint of ale. Charlie was a little edgy about trying alcohol, but everyone else was drinking ale. They took their glasses of the dark brew and paraded to Mark's table. They took a seat, flanking the ladies.

"Yes," began Felix, "you should have seen Mark there draw a bead on those Jerries."

"Yep," agreed Charlie, "that boy is a real hero."

"Ohhh," cooed the two women in unison.

Mark looked a little uncomfortable for only a second, then recovered. "Yep, I am known as the best shot in the outfit." He leaned back in his chair. "They have started calling me Dead-Eye."

"Ohhh," fawned the blond, "Dead-Eye." She smiled at Mark then looked toward the brunette and raised her eyebrows.

"What does that mean?" inquired the brunette.

Mark looked at Charlie and Felix with a blank, confused expression.

"It means he is a really great shot," explained Charlie.

Felix grinned widely. "Yeah. He's great."

Before the evening was over, Charlie had finished his ale and quaffed two more. Felix had to help him walk back to his quarters.

Roshven was a small town on a small island on the western coast of Scotland. The next several months were spent practicing and perfecting amphibious landings.

# CHAPTER 8

"CAN YOU CONNECT me to my parents, Suzie?" entreated Lucy.

"Sure, hon. Hold for a moment," responded Suzie, the switchboard operator.

There was static on the line for a few seconds. Then another voice came on the line.

"Hello there" came Carl Sr.'s voice. "Speak up, I can't hear you."

"I haven't said anything yet, Daddy," yelled Lucy.

"Hello, Lucy. You getting any snow down your way?"

"Daddy, I only live a half mile from you. And yes, it is snowing. In fact, the snow is coming down sideways," commented Lucy.

"Yeah, this wind is driving everyone crazy," howled Carl.

"Who is 'Everyone'?" quizzed Lucy.

"Well, your mother and I," confessed Carl.

"Dad," began Lucy, "I think I have a little water leak."

"Didn't you leave the faucet partially open?" questioned Carl. "Well, I'll be down when the snow lets up a little. Meantime, leave the water running a little."

"The water doesn't really run, Daddy," complained Lucy.

"Well, I'll be down in a bit."

Lucy put the earpiece back on the cradle. She then set the phone back on the small table. She walked into the kitchen and poured herself a cup of coffee. Her long strawberry hair was pulled up into a bun. She took the cup of coffee to the table and sat down.

"I wonder what Charlie is doing," wondered Lucy aloud.

Carl Sr. arrived and found Lucy lost in thought.

"What are you doing, sweetheart?" greeted Carl.

Lucy looked up, startled. "I was just thinking."

"What about?"

Lucy stood without answering. Carl knew she was worried by her silence. He walked to the sink in the kitchen located almost across from the front door.

"The cold water is open all the way, but I am getting only a trickle," explained Lucy.

"Well, let's take a look." Carl kneeled on the floor and opened the cabinet under the sink. He stared at the pipes. He studied it for several minutes then stood.

"Well, I need to go to the truck and get some tools. Where's the little angel?" said Carl.

"She's asleep," responded Lucy without looking up.

"I may need to go to town for some more pipes," stated Carl.

Lucy looked up at him. "I can't afford much."

"Don't worry about. I'll take care of it," assured Carl. "Why is it so cold in here?"

"I ran out of wood yesterday. Can't heat the house without wood to burn," explained Lucy.

A long, harsh cough came from the other room.

"What was that?" questioned Carl.

"Pearl. She has had a cough for a couple of days," explained Lucy.

"Well, no wonder, with this cold," observed Carl. "OK. I will bring you some wood from town to last a day or two. Then I will bring more later."

Tears rolled down Lucy's cheeks. "I'm sorry, Daddy. I am really trying. It's just that Charlie doesn't get paid much though he sends almost all to me. I am just having a hard time."

"It is a tough winter," reassured Carl. "But Charlie is doing his duty. I will help." He shook his head. "I was in the trenches once, you know."

"Thank you, Daddy," Lucy said softly.

"Bundle Pearl up. We need to take her to see the doctor." commanded Carl.

"But—"

"No buts. Just bundle her up. Doc Allison will be happy to see her," reassured Carl.

Carl loaded Lucy and Pearl in his truck and slid through the snowy, muddy road to the doctor's office. He left Lucy and Pearl at the office then went to the Golden Rule General Store. He got some galvanized pipe and then went to see Lester. Lester told him about Jim Stewart, who had a cord of wood for sale. Carl then went to see Jim and bought a cord of wood, which he loaded into the bed of the truck.

He then returned to Doc Allison's office. When he went in, he found Lucy and the baby were in an exam room, so he took a chair and waited. After about five minutes, Lucy came into the waiting room.

"Dr. Allison says Pearl is real sick and needs to stay in the hospital for a few days," explained Lucy. "I will try to work out a payment plan with him, and I will stay with her."

"OK. I will go to your house and get things ready for your return," encouraged Carl.

Lucy went back into the back where Pearl was. Carl walked up to the desk where the nurse sat.

"May I use your phone to call home and let Erin know what is going on?" he politely asked.

"Certainly, sir." The nurse then put the phone on the desk in front of him.

Carl lifted the phone and lifted the earpiece. He clicked the hanger several times to get the operator.

"Hello," he said into the mouthpiece. "Is that you?" He paused a minute, listening. "Can you connect me to my house, Suzie? Yes. I am at the doctor's office . . . No, nothing is wrong. Pearl is just a little sick . . . Thank you." He smiled at the nurse as he waited for Erin to answer.

When Erin did answer, he explained what was going on and that he would be home later. He then left and went back to Lucy's house to fix the plumbing and unload the wood.

"Your daughter has pneumonia. She is going to need to stay here for about two to three days," explained Dr. Allison.

"But I don't know how I will pay for that." Lucy sniffed.

"Tell you what," drawled Dr. Allison, "you come in and clean the office four days a week for a month, and we will call it good. After all, Charlie is off fighting the Nazis."

"But will that be enough?"

"We will call it my contribution to the war effort." Dr. Allison smiled.

"Thank you, sir," acknowledged Lucy.

"I'll have the nurse fix you a bed so you can sleep in the same room with Pearl," elucidated Dr. Allison.

Lucy just nodded.

Dr. Allison leaned forward. "Have you heard from Charlie?"

"He is with the rangers," explained Lucy. "He is still in training in Scotland, I think."

"And what about Carl Jr.?" asked the doctor.

"He is also in Scotland. He is with the infantry," replied Lucy.

"Good," responded the doctor. "Please keep me posted."

"Yes, sir," acquiesced Lucy.

# CHAPTER 9

"IT IS REALLY hot," commented Mark White.

"Shut up," hissed Felix. "And pull the shelter over your hole."

"Yeah," grunted Mark, pulling the tent half over his head and position.

"Charlie?" whispered Mark.

"Shut up," replied Charlie.

"Just lettin' you know the day after tomorrow is Valentine's Day," retorted Mark. "Did you send something to your wife?"

"Shut up," muttered Charlie. "Did you tape your dog tags together?"

"Yep." Mark remained quiet for a full minute. "Well, did you?'

"What?"

"Did you send your wife something for Valentine's Day?" rejoined Mark.

"I'll write her a letter when we get a breather," wheezed Charlie.

Another five minutes passed.

"It is hot," whined Mark.

"For the last time, shut up," instructed Felix quietly. "It will be cool when the sun goes down."

Indeed, when the sun did go down, it became almost cold. Mark was asleep and did not say anything about it.

After the moon set, the order was given quietly, and the men moved out. They moved quickly and silently. When dawn broke, Charlie found they were in a saddle with towering cliffs on either side. The men halted and hunkered down for the day.

Charlie was on the left edge, and just after dark, he heard loud voices speaking German. He and four others slithered toward the noise and found a small patrol of German soldiers. They crept quickly and silently behind the men. Charlie picked a man out and concentrated on him. He stood straight and moved quickly, coming up behind the man. He reached around with his left hand and covered the man's mouth. With his right hand, he brought the razor-sharp combat knife across the man's throat. There was no sound. The man slumped to the ground, spurting blood from his slit throat.

The whole battalion then advanced on the Italian position. Charlie was still on the left but not the very end. He had trotted a hundred yards when he heard firing from his front. Before he could get his M1 Garand to his shoulder, he heard a Thompson submachine gun rat-tat-tat to his right. He aimed to his front and fired. He did not have a definite target but fired to put the enemy's head down. Within minutes he was in the Italian position. He fired the Garand once then began slashing with his bayonet.

He met up with Felix. "You OK?"

"Yeah. Just a little bloody," returned Felix.

"Yours or theirs?" questioned Charlie.

"Not mine."

"You seen Mark?" questioned Charlie.

"Just over there." Felix hitched a thumb over his right shoulder. "He's fine."

Mark saw them and walked over.

"What is this place?" challenged Mark.

"Called Sened Station," replied Felix.

"Huh," grunted Mark.

"Well, we passed our baptism of fire," remarked Charlie.

"Yep," agreed Felix, lighting a cigarette.

"We had that when we came ashore at Oran," stated Mark.

"No, that was nothing. The French had no fight in them," disagreed Charlie, lighting a cigarette.

"Yep," repeated Felix.

The next day, they rested at Gafsa. Charlie sipped on some contraband schnapps and wrote his Valentine's letter to Lucy.

"Dear Lucy," he wrote. "I don't know how much of this will make it past the censors, so will make it short. We are resting today after three days of hard marching." He decided she did not need to know about any of the fighting. That would just worry her. "It is very hot here during the day but gets really cold at night." He sipped some more schnapps. "Marched hard this past week. Have lost some weight but am doing OK. Just wanted to send you a note and tell you how much I love you—though there are not enough words for that—and happy

Valentine's Day." That was all he could think of. That and the German whose throat he had cut. And the one ranger who had his head blown off. So he finished. "Anyway, I love you and miss you terribly." He signed the letter and put it into the addressed envelope.

He took another swig of schnapps and wandered off to find the corporal who handled the mail.

He returned and found Felix and Mark relaxing in the shade of a tent.

"You'll be happy to know I just sent a Valentine's letter to my wife," commented Charlie.

"Proud of you," declared Mark. "Here, have a drink."

"What is it?" asked Charlie.

"Don't ask, just drink it." Felix laughed. "Got a cigarette?"

"Yeah, here," rejoined Charlie, tossing him a cigarette.

# CHAPTER 10

CARL SR. HAD left Lucy with a little money, so she went to the Golden Rule General Store for some King Leo peppermint sticks.

"Good morning, Ms. Morgan," greeted the clerk when she walked in.

"Do I know you?" she asked.

"I have seen you in here several times," responded Alexander Schmidt. He smiled. "I am Alex Schmidt."

"Oh," replied Lucy.

"Yes, ma'am. Is there anything I can help you with?" questioned Alex.

"Do you have some King Leo peppermint sticks?"

"Yes, ma'am. Follow me," instructed Alex.

Alex was average height with dark hair that caressed his ears. He was Lucy's age, with a muscular build.

As he walked, he turned his head back toward Lucy. "I was in school with you, but I don't think you would remember me."

"Oh, why not?" quizzed Lucy.

"I was always buried in my books. I really didn't have time for people."

"Are you the boy who was a whiz at math?" wondered Lucy.

"Yep, that was me," confessed Alex. "I mean, yes, ma'am." He looked around. "I sure hope the boss didn't hear me. He insists we say *ma'am* and *sir* to customers." He turned to face her and pointed to his right. "Here we are."

"Thank you," said Lucy as she took a tin of King Leo peppermints. It was in a circular blue can with a lion printed in white on the side.

"Anything else, ma'am?" asked Alex.

"No, thank you." She looked down shyly. "It is for my daughter, who is in the hospital right now." She giggled. "And for me."

"Maybe I could buy you a burger at the diner. Just to hash over old times." Alex grinned.

"I am married," stated Lucy.

"Just to hash over old times." Alex smiled.

"Maybe," agreed Lucy.

Lucy followed him to the cash register. She paid for the peppermints and walked out, clutching the sack and smiling.

That night, Lucy told the nurse that she would eat out. She pulled her coat around her neck to protect from the ever-present wind and walked to the diner. She walked in as the small bell above the door tinkled, alerting the workers that another customer was there.

"Just sit anywhere you want, hon," sang out a portly woman from behind the counter.

Lucy looked around and noticed there was no one else there except for one older rancher. Somewhat disappointed, she unbuttoned her coat, walked to a small table, and sat down.

"What can I get for you?" questioned the ample woman from behind the counter.

"A burger please," responded Lucy.

"You want any fries?"

"No, thank you."

The waitress straightened up and walked into the back to give her order to the cook.

Lucy looked around. She wasn't sure if she was disappointed or relieved that Alex wasn't there.

The door opened, and the bell tinkled. In walked Suzie, having just been relieved at the switchboard.

"Hello, Lucy. How is Pearl doing?" asked Suzie. She was only about five feet two inches tall and almost that wide. She always wore dresses that draped over her more-than-sufficient body.

"She is doing a little better. Dr. Allison says she should get out of the hospital in a day or two," replied Lucy.

The waitress brought her burger, and Lucy ate it hastily. She was glad to pay her bill and leave. She felt she had betrayed Pearl, leaving her at the hospital. But under that, she had been worried that Alex might actually show up and Suzie would spread rumors all over town.

The next morning, she laid Pearl down for her nap and found herself wondering what she needed from the general store. *I could really use some gum,* thought Lucy. Then she realized what she was doing. She was really thinking of the young man with the dark hair. She remembered the prominent dimple in his chin. The fullness of his lips. She realized she was starting to perspire. She walked to the window and felt the cold seeping through the pane. It was refreshing.

"Are you doing all right?" inquired the nurse, walking in.

"I am fine. I just need some air," countered Lucy. She took her coat from the hanger and started toward the door. "Pearl is sleeping, so I am going to get some air."

"Why don't you go to the diner for some coffee?" wondered the nurse.

"That sounds good," agreed Lucy. She buttoned her coat as she walked out the front door. She walked down the street, walking at an angle into the wind. She walked into the diner with the tinkle of the bell. There was a different waitress with perfectly coiffed white hair.

"Sit where you want. I'll be with you in a minute."

The café was busier than it had been the night before. She found a table at the back that was empty. She unbuttoned her coat as she walked to the table.

She heard the bell tinkle again and looked at the door. It was Alex. She watched him silently as he sauntered to the bar.

"A cup of coffee to go, please, Gloria," sang Alex in his lilting voice.

He was wearing jeans that hugged his small waist and formed across his firm buttocks. His shoulders were broad and muscular. His back was turned to Lucy, but she could almost see the broad grin with perfect teeth.

Lucy dropped her head and felt the flush rise to her cheeks. She could barely suppress a girlish giggle. Perhaps he would look better in some chinos with front pleats.

She was startled by a voice beside her.

"You want some breakfast?" asked the waitress. "Sorry I took so long. I had another customer."

"Yes . . . I mean, no, I don't want any breakfast. Just a cup of coffee, thank you." Lucy blushed.

Lucy drank her coffee, lost in thought. People came and went, but she didn't notice. She was so confused. Alex was a breath of fresh air. But Charlie was her husband, and he was at parts unknown, facing deathly danger.

Lucy shook her head, her lank long hair brushing across her shoulders. She realized her thinking was all wrong. Alex was just a breath of fresh air while Charlie was the air itself. Alex was just a boy, and Charlie was a man. Charlie was her man. Charlie was putting his life on the line to stop the advance of Hitler. Once more, Lucy shook her head. She really did not know who Hitler was or why he needed to be stopped. But everyone said he needed to be stopped, so that must be right.

She got up and walked to the counter. She absently placed a quarter on the counter. The waitress, Gloria, gave her the change, and Lucy put it in her purse. She walked outside, pulling the collar of her coat up around her neck to block the wind. She walked back to the hospital, lost in her thoughts.

She arrived at the hospital and walked in, brushing blown snow from her jacket. She strode to Pearl's room and placed her jacket on a hanger. She then placed it in the closet. She turned to face the bassinet and saw Pearl sitting up sucking on a bottle.

"Did you get some fresh air?" questioned the nurse, bustling into the room.

"Why, yes, thank you," responded Lucy with a slight blush. What did she mean by that? Was she guilty of something, and did it show?

"Well, the little angel is doing fine. She certainly eats very well." The nurse grinned.

"Yes. She has an appetite enough for both of us," squeaked Lucy. Lucy sat in a chair beside the crib.

The nurse left the room and was gone for only a few minutes when she returned. In her hands was a small package wrapped in colorful paper. "This came for you about five minutes ago," pronounced the nurse.

"Thank you." Lucy nodded, taking the package. She opened the package and found a small stuffed bear.

The card read, "For Ms. Morgan. I hope you feel better real soon." It was signed Alex Schmidt.

Pearl was standing in the crib, leaning against the rail for support. She held her hands out toward Lucy and yelled, "Mommy . . . toy."

Lucy looked at Pearl then back at the bear. She was not sure of the full intent of the present, but Pearl would not be denied. Lucy felt the blood rush to her cheeks as she gave the stuffed bear to Pearl.

Pearl played with the bear until lunch arrived. She ate well and then began yawning. Her cough seemed to be improving every hour. About four in the afternoon, Dr. Allison entered the room.

"Well, my dear, I think the little one is on the mend," announced the doctor. "I believe she will be ready to go home tomorrow."

"I can't thank you enough, Dr. Allison," praised Lucy.

A few weeks later, Lucy received a letter from Charlie. It was postmarked February 17, 1943.

> *Well, darling, we have moved into the war. I cannot tell you when or where even if I knew. But it is very exciting. I love you and hope you have a wonderful Valentine's Day. My heart and kisses are with you and Pearl. Please give her a hug and kiss for me.*
>
> *Love,*
> *Charlie*

She read it three times then put it in a safe place for future reference.

# CHAPTER 11

A FTER FEEDING THE horses, Lucy packed Pearl up with her finest lace dress and placed her in the old truck. She then loaded the picnic basket in the truck and took off for town. She arrived at the park and unloaded. She spread a blanket on the grass and went back to the truck. She picked Pearl up in one arm and grabbed the picnic basket with the other. She returned to the blanket and placed nineteen-month-old Pearl on the edge of the blanket.

"Horsey, Mommy." Pearl chortled as an older man walked past with a large dog on a leash.

"No, dear, that is a doggie." Lucy laughed.

"Doggie?" repeated Pearl, amazed.

"Yes, dear," affirmed Lucy. She smiled and leaned back, basking in the sun.

"Kinda warm today" came a voice from behind Lucy.

Lucy turned around to see Alex. He was smiling widely. He had on a white shirt, blue jeans, and a wide brimmed hat.

"It usually is in July," returned Lucy coldly.

"Yep. Usually is," observed Alex.

"You come to the park often?" interrogated Lucy. She stood and self-consciously smoothed her freshly pressed dress.

"Every chance I get." Alex beamed. His perfectly white teeth glinted in the sun.

"I see," countered Lucy, warming a bit.

"May I join you?" inquired Alex.

Pearl giggled brightly and held her arms toward Alex.

"Smart kid," complimented Alex.

"Yes, she is." Lucy smiled. She turned and tilted her head so the sun would catch the color of her auburn hair just right. "And yes, you may join us. Actually, I packed an extra sandwich."

Just then, the old man with the dog walked by and stopped short. "Lucy? Lucy Johansson?"

"Lucy Morgan now, sir," replied Lucy.

The old man looked closely at Alex. "You are Alex Schmidt, aren't you?" interrogated Mr. Johnson.

"Yes, sir." Alex nodded.

Mr. Johnson looked from Alex to Lucy and back to Alex. "She's married, you know."

"Yes, sir, I know. We are just friends," explained Alex.

"Uh-huh," grunted Mr. Johnson. He turned back to Lucy. "You heard from Charlie?"

"Just a few letters. From what I can tell, he is in North Africa, but that is actually classified," confided Lucy. She shuffled her feet.

"How is the stallion?"

"He is fine. He actually seems to miss Charlie," answered Lucy. "He went off his feed for almost a week when Charlie left, but he is much better now."

"Do you ride him any?" quizzed Mr. Johnson.

"No, sir. He is too much horse for me." Lucy fidgeted again. "Junior rode him some after Charlie left, but now Junior is gone to the war too."

"Is this Pearl?" Mr. Johnson did not wait for an answer. "She has grown a mile. How old is she now?"

"She is nineteen months now."

"My, my. Well"—Mr. Johnson looked around—"I must be on my way."

He walked off briskly. When he had disappeared from sight, Lucy and Alex burst out laughing. Lucy realized she had laid her face against Alex's shoulder and he had placed his arms around her. She embarrassedly stepped back, breaking the embrace. But with the realization of that brief intimacy, she felt a strange tingle.

"I'm sorry, Mr. Schmidt, I don't know what got into me," stammered Lucy.

"It is quite all right, Mrs. Morgan. It was strictly innocent." Alex smiled, licking his lips sensuously.

Lucy shook her head and looked around. Pearl had wandered off several baby steps. She laughed, feeling a girlish fire in her belly as she took a step toward Pearl. Pearl saw her advance and began baby-running away. Lucy laughed harder as she chased after the giggling baby.

"How are things at the Golden Rule?" inquired Lucy.

"Fine," replied Alex. "Actually, I am leaving in a couple of months."

Lucy's heart fell to her feet. "Leaving?"

"Yes. I am going to college in Denver."

"Denver?" gasped Lucy.

"I am going to study to be an aeronautical engineer," confessed Alex.

"Oh," sighed Lucy. "You will be a great one."

They sat on the blanket, and Lucy passed around some plates. She spooned some baby food onto Pearl's plate. Then she placed a sandwich and some potato salad on Alex's plate. She then fixed her own plate. They ate in silence. Lucy barely touched her sandwich. Somehow, her appetite had left her.

"I will still be around," explained Alex.

"I don't care," Lucy returned. She tossed her head. "I am married, you know."

"Yes, I know. But I will be coming back to see my parents from time to time," asserted Alex.

"Yes."

Alex took the last bite of his sandwich. "This sandwich is great," he mumbled with a full mouth. He gulped the last down.

"Don't try to change the subject," asserted Lucy.

"No, I'm not. I mean this sandwich is really good. You should think about selling them." Alex nodded.

"I wouldn't know how to go about it," stammered Lucy.

"You know, set up a stand. The guys are haying now. Then they will be bringing in the beets in the fall and feeding livestock in the winter. They always need a quick, easy lunch," encouraged Alex.

"I couldn't," Lucy protested lamely. She looked at Pearl. Pearl yawned largely. "I need to lay Pearl down for a nap."

"OK. But admit it, it is a good idea," said Alex.

Lucy looked at Alex with green eyes that seemed to slowly turn to turquoise. She stared for a full minute. "OK. Yes. It is a good idea."

Alex looked at his watch. "I gotta go get ready for work." He quickly stood up.

"It's Saturday." Lucy cocked her head. "You work on Saturday?"

"Sometimes," replied Alex.

"Yeah, I need to get Pearl home too." Lucy stood. "I will think about the sandwiches."

"I will think about you."

Lucy blushed. "I will too."

Alex leaned forward and kissed her. Their arms circled their bodies, and they became as one for many seconds. Alex pulled back, smiled at Lucy, and turned and quickly left.

Lucy watched Alex walk away, tingling with the thrill of the kiss. As he passed from sight, the heavy pall of guilt fell upon her.

# CHAPTER 12

"**P**UT YOUR HELMET back on, Private!" commanded Staff Sergeant Anderson.

"But it bounces on my head," argued Byron Lawton Wallace.

"Cinch up the chin strap tight and it won't bounce," directed the sergeant.

Byron was a new recruit. A replacement for one of the men lost at Kasserine Pass. He was a six-foot-one-inch-tall Texan with a definite Texas drawl. His hair was blond, and his ears stuck out from the sides of his head. Thus, he had earned the nickname Ears in his short time with the rangers.

Charlie leaned his rifle against his left shoulder and leaned over and helped Ears buckle his helmet.

"Unbuckle it as soon as you hit the beach," yelled Charlie over the noise of the diesel engines of the LCI.

Ears nodded solemnly, eyes remaining steadily to the front.

It was shortly after midnight, and the LCIs were tossed mercilessly by the forty-mile-per-hour winds. The boats were having a difficult time following the guide boat in the heavy seas and nighttime darkness. The trip seemed to last forever. But eventually, the sound of the diesel engines began to get quieter as the boats slowed.

The front ramp fell with a splash into the shallow surf. The men rapidly exited the LCI with no sound except the splash of boots in the ankle-deep surf and the clank of slings on M1 rifles. This had been practiced several times in Scotland and performed with great success in Algeria, so it was business as usual.

The town of Gela, Sicily, was on a rise from the ocean about 150 feet above the coast. In its front was a pier, which was about two thousand feet wide. Charlie's company of rangers hit the beach to the left of the pier. Further to the left was a fort, which was the target. Charlie ran up the beach a short way then was directed to bear left and keep moving.

Charlie ran about one hundred feet when he heard a deafening explosion. In the graying light, he saw pieces of flesh raining down to his front.

"Minefield!" came shouts from multiple voices at the same time. Almost simultaneous with the shouts were three or four more explosions. The blasts were so close temporally that it was difficult to determine the exact number of eruptions.

Charlie froze in position. Then came the rat-a-tat-tat of machine-gun fire.

"Get down!" yelled Charlie as he fell prone on the ground.

"No!" screamed Sergeant Randall. "On your feet. Take to the right. To the slope."

No sooner had he finished speaking than another detonation occurred, and the sergeant was tossed into the air. The sergeant struggled to his feet and covered the gash in his abdomen with his cartridge belt. He swung and signaled the men to move to the right and up a steep embankment.

At the top of the embankment was a dirt road. Charlie followed the sergeant up the embankment. At the other side of the road was a slight incline, which contained several pillboxes and machine gunners. Charlie lay prone and brought his Garand to bear. He sighted carefully and squeezed the trigger. He saw an Italian soldier throw his hands high in the air, away from the machine gun he had been firing, and fall backward.

Sergeant Randall ran forward across the dirt road, firing ceaselessly with his .45-caliber pistol. He reached the other side and fell on his wounded belly, barely thirty feet from a pillbox. Charlie watched, amazed, as the sergeant pulled a pin on a grenade then tossed it effortlessly into the rectangular opening in the front of the pillbox. There was an intense yet muffled boom from the pillbox as smoke billowed from the rectangular opening.

Charlie moved past Sergeant Randall to the next pillbox and tossed a grenade into the opening.

Ears passed Charlie and ran to the next pillbox. He pulled the pin on the grenade as he saw the machine-gun-muzzle flash blare from the forward opening. He gritted his teeth and tossed the grenade into the concrete box.

In less than two hours, the whole line of machine guns and pillboxes had been neutralized.

Charlie leaned against the dirt embankment and lit a cigarette. He wiped sweat from his forehead as he exhaled a puff of blue smoke.

A lieutenant walked down the dirt road and glanced over at the embankment. Not ten feet away sat Sergeant Randall. The lieutenant noticed the blood seeping from under the cartridge belt Randall had tied around his middle.

"You are injured, Sergeant," snapped the lieutenant.

"Yes, sir, I am." Randall nodded. "Slightly."

"Let me see," ordered the lieutenant.

Randall removed the cartridge belt. The lieutenant took a half step back. He turned and yelled, "I need two men to get this man to an aid station." He looked around. "You and you, make a stretcher."

Randall replaced the cartridge belt. "No, sir, I'm not helpless yet. Get me some prisoners to guard or something."

The lieutenant stared at him for a long moment. Then he looked down and shook his head. "Carry on, soldier,"

Ears looked at Charlie. "Is it always like this?" he questioned.

"Nope," replied Charlie. "Usually, it's worse."

Ears stood and looked around. "Sure could be a pretty place," he commented.

A burst of machine-gun fire sounded from the brush to the north of the road. Ears sat down quickly, and Charlie lay back and rolled over on his belly, bringing his rifle to bear. Several shots rang out from the ranger line, and the machine-gun fire stopped.

Charlie rolled on his back and lit another cigarette.

Ears let out a grand sigh. Charlie inhaled the smoke from his cigarette and looked over at Ears. He exhaled quickly as he saw Ears sitting with writhing intestines in his lap. The intestines steamed and moved slowly as gas and digested food slid through the tube.

"Ears!" yelled Charlie.

Ears looked at Charlie. "I think I am going to die," he commented modestly.

"No, Ears," commanded Charlie. "Medic!" he yelled.

Ears looked Charlie in the eyes. "It ain't no good," he quietly remarked.

"Medic!" yelled Charlie. "Hang on, Ears."

Ears's mouth opened, but no sound came out—only a glob of frothy blood. That is when Charlie noticed the hole in Ears's field jacket over the right breast.

Charlie looked him in the eyes and saw the life leave his body. Byron Lawton Wallace's body fell back into the Sicilian dust.

A medic arrived. "He is dead," announced the medic.

"Yep," agreed Charlie.

"Move on, soldier," commanded the medic as he removed one of the dog tags.

The rangers soon had the fort under control, and the Italians surrendered.

# CHAPTER 13

"OH FUDGE!" LUCY blurted out as she heard a vehicle drive up. "Who would be coming to visit me just after lunch?"

She bustled about clearing the kitchen of the lunch dishes. Fortunately, she had put Pearl down for a nap ten minutes earlier. She finished getting the dishes in the sink just as there was a light tap at the door. She straightened her hair and took off her apron as she scooted to the door. When she opened the door, she drew in a deep breath. There stood Alex Schmidt. He stood straight with a white linen shirt with the top three buttons undone. He smelled of lilacs and honeysuckle.

"What are you doing here?" Lucy blushed. "I mean, to what do I owe the pleasure of this visit?"

"Um, I was in the neighborhood, and I thought I would stop by," stammered Alex.

"I see," Lucy baited him. She stared at him for a long moment.

"May I come in?" questioned Alex.

"Certainly." Lucy stepped aside, still holding the door. Alex walked in, and she quietly closed the door. She turned back to Alex. "Now, what exactly can I do for you?"

"Nothing." Alex smiled. "That is, I am getting things together to leave for Denver tomorrow." He shuffled his feet. "And I just had to see you again."

Lucy dropped her head to hide the blush of dismay. "I will miss you."

"You hardly know me," stated Alex flatly.

"I know," responded Lucy.

"Where is Pearl?"

"She is asleep. Taking a nap," explained Lucy.

Alex took a step toward her. Lucy did not move away.

"I am excited to study in the big city, but I wish I had found you earlier," Alex uttered.

"Me too," answered Lucy, still looking down.

Alex put his fingers under Lucy's chin and lifted her head up. "You are so beautiful."

Lucy brushed at the wrinkles in her housedress. She felt as if she had been continually embarrassed since Alex had arrived. "I'm just plain ol' Lucy."

"No, you are heavenly," complimented Alex. He reached out and put his arms around her, drawing her close.

Lucy smelled the freshly washed linen with the slight hint of male sweat. She felt the heavy, well-muscled chest against her breasts. She felt as if she would never be able to catch her breath. She felt his firm, soft cheek press against hers. She felt his firm manhood press against her womanhood.

Alex leaned his head forward and looked deeply into her eyes. In an instant, their lips met, and they kissed passionately. Urgently, Lucy unbuttoned his shirt and pulled it off his shoulders. Alex kissed her as he unbuttoned the front of her housedress and pulled it from her shoulders. The dress fell to the ground without a sound. She pressed her bare breasts against his chest and lost herself in the ardor. The two shuffled to the couch, remaining locked together.

Lucy sat heavily on the couch and unbuttoned his pants. She rapidly uncovered him completely then pulled him on top of her.

An hour later, they were sitting at the kitchen table, dressed again. Lucy lit two cigarettes and handed one to Alex. He took it and puffed easily on it.

"Wow! That was wonderful," exclaimed Alex.

"Hush," cautioned Lucy, "don't wake the baby." She took another puff of her cigarette. She exhaled the smoke slowly. "You know that can never happen again."

"But I love you," protested Alex.

"And I love you. But I also love Charlie, and I am married to him." Lucy took another puff.

"Leave him. Come with me to Denver."

"I cannot leave here. And I cannot leave Charlie," corrected Lucy.

"Well, I have to go to Denver in the morning," announced Alex.

"I know," Lucy said softly. She heard a rustle from the other room. "You better leave before Pearl wakes up."

"Will you write me?" questioned Alex.

"Maybe. That is the best answer I can give you right now," uttered Lucy without lifting her head.

"Look at me just once more so that I can remember those bright blue eyes," pleaded Alex.

Lucy looked at him. Her eyes twinkled, but there was a deep hurt that Alex could see deep within.

Alex stood. "Then this is good-bye?"

"Yes," responded Lucy.

Alex took her in his arms again. Lucy did not resist. He kissed her intensely then released her, turned, and left without looking back.

Lucy sat down awkwardly and cried with her face buried in her hands. The cool September winds blew heavy clouds across the darkening sky.

Pearl woke up and began to cry. Lucy sat at the kitchen table and gazed out the window at the dark sky. It was right out of a novel—a pathetic fallacy. After a few minutes, she slowly arose and went in to pick Pearl up and give her another bottle.

# CHAPTER 14

ONCE MORE, CHARLIE kneeled in a landing craft—this time, not thrown about as much as before. It was still dark, and the sea was relatively quiet. There were many more new faces this time, but Charlie did not feel it was his job to teach them. They should have learned all this stuff already. He didn't even look at their faces. They were just new bodies.

"Be careful. Watch for mines. Keep your heads down," yelled the lieutenant.

The front ramp fell, and the rangers quietly, quickly, and efficiently exited the LCI into the surf. There were no flashes of light. There were no sounds of explosions or rifle fire. Just the quiet of predawn.

Charlie ran quickly yet carefully across the beach. He ran about one hundred yards and fell flat on his belly, rifle at the ready. Still, there were no gun flashes or the crack of rifle fire. He stood and ran the final stretch across the beach. He sat down and leaned against a tree. He lit a cigarette, cupping his hands around the flame to hide the glow. Felix slid up and plopped down beside him.

"Got another?" inquired Felix.

"Here," answered Charlie, thumping a cigarette from the pack. He held it out toward Felix, who took it. Charlie returned the pack to the chest pocket of his jacket. "What now?"

"We keep moving until they show some interest." Felix grinned.

"Well, let's finish these fags first," grunted Charlie.

When they had finished the cigarettes, they lined up with the others and moved forward down an uneven road. They moved in line up the side of the road as dawn began to fully break.

"Word is, we are moving toward the Ciunizi Pass," informed Felix as they walked.

"Where is that?" demanded Charlie.

"In Italy." Felix pointed forward. "Somewhere up that way."

The men marched silently uphill. The ground around the road was scattered with boulders. Charlie kept his eyes on the boulders and the area around them. If the Germans showed up, it would be around some of the boulders. Any boulders not occupied by Germans would make good cover.

Suddenly, the line came to a halt. Charlie was close to the front of the line and had a good look at where the lieutenant was kneeling. The lieutenant motioned to a soldier behind him. The soldier quickly moved to his side, remaining low the whole way. There was a quick exchange between the two. Charlie read the hand signals. There was something just ahead. The lieutenant turned and motioned to the group. The men spread out to the sides among the boulders. Only one man remained on each side of the road.

The men moved forward slowly. Charlie was just off the road. He moved quickly but watched where he placed his feet so that he did not make any sound.

Charlie heard voices from just ahead.

"*Sheisen!*"

"*Vas ist los?*"

"*Vo ist die corporal?*"

Then Charlie saw them. There was a German Volkswagen patrol car. There were four men in gray-green uniforms standing around it.

Charlie aimed at the first one. He took two gentle steps forward, rifle at the ready.

"Drop your weapons," shouted the lieutenant.

The Germans pulled up their weapons, and Charlie fired. The German he was aiming at fell with blood seeping from his shoulder. The other Germans, somewhat confused, fired wildly, hitting no one.

"Drop your weapons!" repeated the lieutenant.

The Germans dropped their guns and raised their hands. The rangers ran forward and took the Germans prisoner. The medic hurried to the German whom Charlie had wounded and began taking care of him.

The men heard a rustle in the brush just on the other side of the boulders.

"*Warum schiessen sie?*"

The lieutenant held his hand up. The men waited, weapons pointed toward the voice. Soon, three more Germans came through the brush.

"Drop your weapons!" yelled the lieutenant.

"*Lassen sie ihre waffen fallen!*" yelled one of the captured Germans.

The lieutenant looked at the German who had just spoken as two of the rangers moved forward and relieved the newcomers of their weapons.

"So you speak English?" interrogated the lieutenant.

"*Ein bisschen* . . . a little," responded the German who had spoken.

"Gather 'em up, boys," commanded the lieutenant.

The lieutenant detailed two men to escort the fourteen prisoners to the rear echelon.

"Let's move, gentlemen," announced the lieutenant.

Charlie moved out with the others. They continued up the mountain road until they reached a small plateau. Charlie was thrilled at the sight of the land spreading out in front of and behind him. They moved to the right of the road and began to set about, digging slit trenches and other defensive measures.

"Martin!" called out the lieutenant.

Soon the radio operator came up and slid down beside the lieutenant. The lieutenant looked at his map then studied the plain that stretched out in front of them.

"Call in naval fire at these coordinates," barked the lieutenant to the radioman. He pointed to some pencil scribbles on the map.

Soon the scream of artillery shells flying just over the rangers' heads broke the silence. Charlie could see the Germans walking around on the plain. There appeared puffs of white smoke among the Germans, and some of them fell. Charlie grinned as he watched them running about randomly.

"Hold your fire. It's ours," shouted the lieutenant as one of the rangers fired two shots with his M1.

Charlie turned around and looked out at the Gulf of Salerno. Ships filled the ocean. He could see the battleship, which was shelling the Germans in front of him.

When darkness fell, Charlie was nearing exhaustion. He took the first watch and crawled about fifty feet in front of the line. He found a stunted tree growing beside a large boulder and settled in for his two-hour stint. Charlie had been sweating all day. Now, with the sun down, he was getting chilled.

"Hisst!" came a hiss from behind Charlie. Charlie turned with his M1 at the ready.

"Smoke," whispered Charlie hoarsely.

"Fire" was the answer. "Where are you?"

"Just to the left of your front."

Seconds later, Charlie's relief showed up.

"Got a fag?" questioned Charlie.

"Yeah," replied Morris Carson.

Morris was short and stocky but not fat. He was only five feet four inches tall but tough as nails. But most of the men found his name too long and called him Less. He earned that name because of his height, not his effort. His best friend, Jake, was over six feet tall and was nicknamed More. It worked because when the lieutenant needed a volunteer, he would yell "More or Less!" which he did as often as possible.

Charlie went back to his slit trench and snuggled in. He could not find a comfortable place or find a comfortable position for his aching legs. Still, he slept fitfully until dawn.

He was jarred awake to the sharp chatter of gunfire. He pulled his M1 to the edge of the trench and peered over. There were Germans running through the boulders toward the ranger position. The enemy was less than a hundred yards away, and Charlie sighted carefully. He rapidly squeezed the trigger, and a German fell. He barely saw him fall before he was sighting on the next one. Before he could pull the trigger, the German fell behind a large rock and began firing. Instinctively, Charlie ducked though he was not sighted in by this enemy. Charlie took a deep breath and aimed for the helmet sticking out beside the rock. He held his breath and pulled slowly on the trigger. The M1 fired, and the German fell beside the rock.

The firing continued for thirty minutes with only an occasional target. Then it appeared to be over. Charlie leaned back in his trench and lit a cigarette.

"You there, Felix?" shouted Charlie.

"Yeah. You OK?" came the answer.

"Yeah. About out of smokes though," complained Charlie.

"Me too," responded Felix.

"How you doing on food?" asked Charlie.

"Not too good. More food than smokes, though," commented Felix.

"Me too," repeated Charlie.

"Water?" questioned Felix.

"About half a canteen," said Charlie.

"What are we gonna do?" queried Felix.

"Water is more important than food or smokes and easier to find," stated Charlie.

"Where?"

"There's a stream just over that rise," explained Charlie, pointing toward their front.

"But that is where the Germans are," challenged Felix.

"I know. But we gotta have water," elucidated Charlie.

"I'll go," stated Eric Collins, who had been listening from the next trench.

"Who is that?" yelled Charlie.

"It's me," stated Eric.

"Take an extra canteen. I'll keep mine just in case," stated Charlie, tossing an empty canteen over to Eric's trench.

Eric was an eighteen-year-old from Wisconsin, where his family ran a dairy farm. He was almost six feet tall with a childish potbelly. He had joined the rangers after Sicily and was with them just in time for the assault on Salerno.

"Be careful, Green Bay," shouted Charlie.

Eric had gained the name Green Bay since he was from Wisconsin, though nowhere near that famous city.

Eric left his trench and ran hunched over toward the front. He had three canteens in his hands, and his M1 Garand rifle slung on his right shoulder.

"Good kid," commented Felix.

"Got a lot to learn, though," returned Charlie.

Thirty minutes later, Charlie was getting worried. He looked over the trench toward the front then toward Felix's trench. "If he's not back in five minutes, I am going to look for him."

Two minutes later, Eric broke through the brush in front of the trenches. He tossed Charlie a full canteen as he slid into his trench. He then looked over the top of his trench and tossed another canteen to Charlie.

"That one's for Felix," stated Eric as he tossed the second canteen.

"What took you so long?" asked Charlie.

"Had a hard time finding the stream. Ain't much water in it. But I guess there was enough," explained Eric.

"Good job, Green Bay," complimented Charlie.

The next morning, Charlie woke and stretched his aching muscles. He found a cigarette butt and lit it. He still had two cigarettes, but he preferred to smoke a butt in the morning as he did not want to spend the time on a full cigarette.

"Here they come!" yelled Felix.

Charlie pushed the butt into the dirt side of the trench and kneeled, looking over the edge of the trench with his M1 at the ready. He saw the "potato masher" hand grenade fly through the air. It appeared to be in slow motion as he saw the explosive arch toward his trench. He rolled out of the back side of the trench. As he left his excavation, the grenade exploded. He rolled twice then slid up to the lip of the trench. He aimed the M1 across the trench, sighted a German, and fired. His aim was true, and the German fell. The attack lasted only a short time, and Charlie slid back into his trench.

Felix vaulted into the trench beside Charlie.

"I'm so tired of this shit," griped Felix as he came to a rest at the front bank of the trench.

"SUSFU," sighed Charlie.

"Yep, situation unchanged, still fucked up." Felix chuckled.

Charlie felt a strong discomfort in his right thigh. He rolled over so he was leaning against the wall of the trench on his left side. "Damn." He swiped at the back of his pants on the right. He felt something wet and sticky. He pulled his hand up and looked at it. "Blood," he stated simply.

"What the hell?" shouted Felix, somewhat alarmed.

"Don't know," responded Charlie.

Felix stuck his head above the lip of the trench. "Medic!" he screamed.

In a few moments, Andy Dickenson fell into the trench. He had a large white armband with a red cross on it tied around his right upper arm.

"What the hell you yellin' about?" he interrogated.

"Charlie's wounded," stated Felix simply.

"Where?" asked Andy.

"Show him, Charlie," commanded Felix.

"I ain't showin' him," refuted Charlie.

"Roll over." Felix frowned, shoving Charlie's shoulder.

Charlie rolled onto his left side. Andy took one look.

"Damn," he cussed. He looked up over the lip of the trench. "I need a stretcher over here!"

"Looks like you got yourself the million-dollar wound," gloated Felix as he handed Charlie a cigarette.

Andy looked over his shoulder at them. "Naw, that's a two-bit wound, at best. He will be out of this for only a couple of months."

Charlie looked from Andy to Felix. "Better than being stuck here with you bums for two months."

Felix only nodded as he lit Charlie's cigarette then lit his own.

# CHAPTER 15

"**G**OOD MORNING, LUCY," greeted Marvin Meyer as he sat in his usual barstool.

"Good morning," returned Lucy as she wiped the counter in front of him. "The usual?"

"Yep." Marvin settled his ample seat onto the stool. "Is the coffee hot?"

"As always," assured Lucy.

"Good. It is cold out there and looking like snow."

"I don't mind the snow so much if it would just come straight down," twittered Lucy.

"Not usually this cold in September," expanded Marvin. "Though I remember one September when the snow started on the fifth and didn't end until April."

"Yep," agreed Lucy as she poured him a cup of coffee. "It is Wyoming, and if you don't like the weather, just wait an hour or two and it will change."

Marvin nodded. "Got a big day ahead. Gotta start haying the cattle already." He looked around the small café. "Sure am glad you opened this place. Best place for a hot meal"—he held up his coffee cup—"and a hot cup of Joe."

"Well, I enjoy it. And it helps with the bills."

"Heard from Charlie lately?" quizzed Marvin.

"Got a letter last week but didn't get much from it. Most of it was just black lines," she explained. She adjusted her apron. "But just knowing he's all right enough to write helps."

"Damn censors. What kind of military secrets is a mere private aware of?" He leaned back, warming to his subject. "Now when I was in France in the first European war, I didn't know nothing except I wanted to stay alive."

"Actually, Charlie is a corporal now," observed Lucy.

"Well, good for him." Marvin grinned at her. "Still, they don't usually tell noncoms nothin'."

"Well, at least he is alive." Lucy sighed.

The bell above the door tinkled as another customer walked in.

"What kind of sandwiches are you selling today?" inquired Cody Brewster as he strolled up to the bar. "Howdy, Marvin."

"Howdy, Cody. Kinda cold out, ain't it?" returned Marvin.

"Yep. But cows gotta be fed, hogs gotta be slopped, and fences still gotta be fixed."

"I have roast beef sandwich today," stated Lucy. "Want one?"

"Yep. Make it to go, please," returned Cody.

Lucy had taken some of Charlie's army pay and began payments on a small place in town. She had a bar with four stools and three tables with four chairs at each table. She had put in a small kitchen in the back and sold breakfast and lunch meals. She made her own bread for the sandwiches and did the cooking herself. She had already built up quite a good clientele.

"You still up at the Palmer ranch?" asked Lucy as she cut two slices of homemade bread and began smearing mayonnaise on it.

"Yep. Gonna be ridin' a lot of fence today," commented Cody.

"Well, I will have this for you in no time," assured Lucy.

"When you gonna get some help?" asked Marvin.

Lucy set a plate with eggs, sausage, and toasted bread in front of Marvin. "I got all the help I can afford right now," stated Lucy.

"You're getting pretty busy here," began Marvin. "You're going to have to get some help before too long."

Lucy wiped her hands on her apron. She looked around. "You might be right." She looked at Cody. "Will have your sandwich ready in a moment."

She returned to the kitchen and wrapped the sandwich in some wax paper. She strode back to the front and handed Cody his sandwich. He paid her and left with the tinkle of the bell.

"You know," said Marvin, speaking around mouthfuls of food, "you have this wall between the dining area and the kitchen. You should knock a hole in the wall and put an opening there. Then hire someone to wait on customers, and all you have to do is cook."

Lucy looked over where Pearl was sitting, playing with her doll. "Yes, that would help a lot." She twisted up her face. "But who could I get to work here? I couldn't pay much at first."

"Get one of the Mexican girls to work here. They are good workers and don't need much," mused Marvin.

"Oh, Marvin, they are just like everyone else," contradicted Lucy.

"Still ought to think about it," mumbled Marvin as he shoved the last bite of bread into his mouth.

"You really need to eat a little more slowly." Lucy laughed. "How can you even taste it?"

"Don't worry." Marvin laughed. "I tasted it, all right. And it was excellent. Real cuisine, just like them French places in 1918."

"Thank you." Lucy beamed. She knew Marvin liked to talk about his time in the service in Europe in the Great War. She thought it was probably because he felt somewhat overshadowed by the current conflict.

Marvin paid his bill and started out. He stopped with his hand on the door and turned around. "You really ought to think about hiring some help. It may be slow now, but just wait. I predict that by Thanksgiving, this place will be hopping."

Marvin worked at the electric company and usually ate breakfast at Lucy's early in the morning. So as he left, the sun was just over the horizon. By ten o'clock, Lucy had served ten people and felt a little frazzled. Still, she had to get prepared for the lunch rush.

She thought about what Marvin had said and, a week later, had Maria Vasquez working for her. She did the cooking, and Maria waited on the customers.

Maria helped Lucy convince her father, Diego, to cut a hole in the wall and place a ledge there. Now, Maria could take the orders to the window, and Lucy could put the plate on the ledge when it was done. Lucy bought a bell from the Golden Rule General Store and would ding it when the order was ready.

There was a large room with four tables and four chairs at each table. The floor was square tiles in a black-and-white checkerboard pattern. There was a counter at the back with a large black cash register. Behind that was a wall with a hole cut in the center to pass the orders. Behind the wall was the kitchen with a large stove and a large white porcelain sink to wash dishes.

The business was a complete success. Lucy's burgers on homemade bread became the talk of the town.

"What are you wearing?" questioned Lucy.

"This is my Halloween costume," replied Maria.

"Halloween is two days away," Lucy pointed out.

"*Sí.* But that is a Sunday. Today is the day for my costume," countered Maria.

"What are you supposed to be?" asked Lucy.

Maria thrust her hip out. "It is not what you think. I am a gypsy."

Lucy studied Maria. She was wearing a long plaid skirt and a white top with the arms pulled down to expose the shoulders. The top plunged to reveal ample cleavage.

"What do you think Mrs. Shepherd will think when she sees that?" interrogated Lucy. Mrs. Thelma Shepherd was the seventy-two-year-old wife of Mr. Orville Shepherd, who was the vice president of one of the local banks. She employed Maria on a part-time basis to clean her house and was very proper and prudish.

"She will think what she wants to think." Maria's lips dropped. "I will tell her I am a gypsy for Halloween."

"OK. But don't wear anything like that again," informed Lucy.

"Yes, ma'am," responded Maria.

# CHAPTER 16

"YOU MADE IT back!" greeted Felix.

"Yep. It will take me a little while to resume the ranger stride," replied Charlie.

"Well, we are in control of Salerno now, and the town is open for R and R," gloated Felix.

"Lead the way." Charlie grinned. Charlie adjusted his Ike jacket and followed Felix. "Thanksgiving in Italy," he commented.

Felix drew up quickly. "Wait. You need to do something first."

Charlie looked around. "What?"

"You've been promoted to sergeant. Murphy bought it at Chiunzi Pass. You need to go by supply and get some stripes," explained Felix.

"Oh yeah, I almost forgot." Charlie unbuttoned his right breast pocket and pulled out a piece of paper. "Here are the orders for my promotion. I almost forgot about it."

"We'll wait here for you, Sarge," stated Felix, lighting a cigarette.

Felix leaned against the wall of the building they were standing beside as Charlie sauntered off. Felix watched him carefully and noted that there was no noticeable limp.

Ten minutes later, Charlie returned with sergeant stripes pinned over his corporal stripes.

"Let's go," invited Charlie.

"Sure," agreed Felix. "Come on."

Felix began wandering down the street, Charlie keeping pace with him.

"Who else did we lose?" inquired Charlie.

"From our company, there was Sergeant Murphy, Mason, and Lyttle killed." He spat on the ground. "Ellis, you, and five others wounded. You are the only one who has returned, so far."

"Damn," Charlie grunted. He continued walking with his friend. "Where are we going?"

"There is a nice bistro just up the street. I figured you could use some food and a little entertainment," expounded Felix.

Soon they were seated in a small restaurant in the shell-pocked town of Salerno, Italy. A very buxom brunette walked over to the table at which they were seated.

"For what can I do you, gentlemen?" asked the brunette.

"Signorina, a little vino please," answered Felix.

"Eat?" asked the brunette.

"*Sì*, pasta with tomato sauce," ordered Felix.

"*Sì, sì, spaghetti con sugo di carne,*" repeated the waitress.

Felix held up two fingers. "Duo," he explained.

"*Sì,*" agreed the brunette waitress as she turned and walked to the kitchen.

"What else you guys been doing while I was being patched up?" inquired Charlie.

"Some training but mostly getting haircuts, shaving, and enjoying the sea breezes," replied Felix. "Scuttlebutt says we are going back into the lines as infantry."

"No," huffed Charlie. "What a waste of training. We were not trained to be plain infantry."

"Yep. If that happens, I am afraid some will transfer out of the outfit," groused Felix.

"Who?" interrogated Charlie.

"I ain't saying," refused Felix.

"You ain't sayin'? Why not?" demanded Charlie.

"You're a sergeant now. I ain't gonna get another ranger in trouble," refused Felix.

"In trouble for what? Transfer ain't no reason for trouble. Every man has a right to ask for transfer."

"True, but you could make life rough on 'em," said Felix.

"Never mind, here comes our food," Charlie acquiesced.

The waitress shuffled up to their table, her shoes shuffling in the debris, which had fallen from the ceiling. She leaned over the table, placing the steaming dishes in front of the two soldiers, her plump breasts straining at her partially unbuttoned shirt.

The two men ate the spaghetti rapidly and silently.

# CHAPTER 17

THE BELL ABOVE the door tinkled as Mark Mayer entered Lucy's shop.

"Hello, Mark," greeted Maria.

"Good morning, Maria," returned Mark. "What's the special this morning?"

"Eggs and bacon with toast—just like every morning," countered Maria.

"Lucy cooking?" asked Mark.

"You ask that every time you come in, and the answer is always the same," snapped Lucy, looking through the order window.

"How you cooking the eggs this morning?" asked Mark.

"Fried, scrambled, or boiled," returned Lucy.

"Fried, thanks," ordered Mark. "How deep's the snow out your way?"

"Was two feet yesterday. I slept here last night. Too much snow to get through," stated Lucy.

"You closing for Christmas?" questioned Mark.

"Yeah. We will be here Christmas Eve until noon," replied Lucy.

"You gonna order or not?" quizzed Maria.

"Yeah, I will have the special," Mark replied. He leaned back in his chair. "Have you heard from Charlie or Carl Jr.?"

"Yes. Carl is in England, and Charlie is somewhere else. Italy, I think."

"You don't know where he is?" questioned Mark.

"Not for sure. The censors butcher his letters, so I don't really know where he is. But I think he is in Italy."

"Is he all right?" asked Mark with unfeigned concern.

Lucy shrugged. "I guess. He wrote." She busied herself with the eggs. "Of course, it was postmarked Thanksgiving."

Just then, Pearl trotted in on unsteady tiny legs.

"Who is this?" inquired Mark.

"Pearl, get back here!" shouted Lucy through the order window.

"So this is Pearl?" Mark grinned as he held his arms out toward the toddler. "So this is the heartbreaker. My, she has grown."

"You just saw her last week." Lucy chuckled as she slid Mark's fried eggs onto the plate.

"Yeah, but she has really grown," stated Mark as he took Pearl into his arms.

Lucy placed the plate with bacon and eggs and two pieces of toasted homemade bread on the shelf at the order window.

"Order up," she shouted a little too loud.

"I can hear you, I'm right here," groused Maria, taking the plate. She walked over and laid it gently down in front of Mark. "Can I get you anything else, sir?"

"Ketchup?" asked Mark.

"Just a minute, sir," cooed Maria.

Maria was totally unpredictable. One minute she was brash and harsh, the next, sweet as sugar. In a very short time, she returned to the table with the ketchup.

"Come here, Pearl. Let the man eat," commanded Lucy from the window.

Pearl, who was very comfortable in Mark's lap, looked at her mother and shouted, "No!"

"Pearl, come here right now!"

"No!"

Lucy bustled out from the kitchen, storming to Mark's table. She grabbed Pearl by the upper arm. "Come with me." She hustled Pearl to the kitchen and sat her down in a small chair, which was pulled up to a small round table. "Now sit there and eat your breakfast."

She turned back to the grill in a huff. She scraped the grill with the end of a metal spatula a little too vigorously.

"Sounds like the little princess has a mind of her own." Mark laughed.

"She certainly is strong willed," agreed Lucy. "With Charlie being halfway around the world and this place being so busy, she is going to be the death of me."

"Has Charlie seen her?" asked Mark.

"He saw her when she was born and, again, when she was about six weeks old. He has been gone since," explained Lucy, talking through the order window.

"Too bad," remarked Mark, shaking his head. "He will be very surprised when he sees her again."

"I just hope he can see her again. So many casualties." Lucy sighed.

Mark paid his bill and left a nice tip for Maria.

"You know, he says the same things every week when he comes in here," Maria called out to Lucy as she cleaned the table.

"Yes, I know. But he is so nice and seems so concerned," answered Lucy. "Besides, he leaves you a good tip."

"Sí. I am not complaining." Maria giggled.

The day was very busy. Many people were in town for Christmas shopping and decided to stop by Lucy's for lunch. Fortunately, Pearl had slept through the majority of the rush. Lucy had heard people talk of the trials of raising a two-year-old, but Pearl was a little too defiant.

# CHAPTER 18

"SERGEANT, GET YOUR men prepared to move out. We board ship in one hour," instructed the lieutenant.

"Yes, sir." Charlie saluted the officer. "May I ask what our orders are?"

"No, you may not. Your only orders are to get your men prepared to board ship."

Charlie saluted again. He did an about-face and hurried off to collect his troops. He could tell by the bustle that something big was happening.

Charlie and his company assembled on the docks of Baia on Pazzouli Bay. They were loaded on transport ships and left the bay about midnight.

The Mediterranean January night was cold and moist. Charlie pulled the collar of his combat jacket about his neck as he walked up the ramp to the troopship.

The next morning, Charlie was "invited" to a briefing. He arrived in the wardroom and found a seat. There was a low rumble of voices as men milled about finding seats.

The lieutenant arrived, and the room was called to attention. Charlie stood straight and stiff, looking straight ahead. He sat back down after an "as you were."

"Gentlemen," began the lieutenant, "we are landing on the shore of Italy at a town called Anzio. It is just south of Rome and is the gateway to Rome and the end of this portion of the conflict." He looked around the room. "When you hit the beach, you are to move quickly inland and set up the beachhead. We expect light resistance. However, you are to advance quickly whether you meet light or heavy resistance. Let me assure you, gentlemen, that this is an extremely important operation, and I expect every man to do his duty."

Charlie leaned over to the sergeant sitting beside him. "Nice speech. Is he a ninety-day wonder?"

"He came in after Salerno was taken," replied the sergeant.

After the briefing, Charlie returned to his company. Felix was the first to corner him.

"What's the plan?" Felix inquired.

"Anzio." He looked at Felix. "I'll tell you more when we get the rest of the men together."

Soon the whole company was assembled. Charlie stood in front of the group.

"We are hitting the beach at a small town just south of Rome called Anzio. When you hit the beach, you are to move quickly inland and consolidate the beachhead," explained Charlie.

"So what's different about this landing?" asked Private Ned Nelson.

"Nothing," agreed Charlie. "It is just like in training, North Africa, Sicily, and Salerno."

"What about enemy deployment?" inquired Felix.

"Good question, Felix." Charlie nodded. "We don't know. It could be very slight or very stiff. But"—he looked around the room—"it doesn't really matter. The rangers will lead the way ashore."

Shortly after midnight the next day, Charlie and his company loaded into LCIs and started toward the docks at Anzio.

Charlie huddled down in the LCI, trying to warm up. The night was black and very cold. He shivered with the cold and waited for the sound of the preliminary artillery salvos. But there was no noise except the sound of the diesel engines of the boats.

They had been in the LCIs for quite some time when he heard the rockets and artillery shells whizz overhead. Within minutes, the bombardment stopped, and a minute later, the ramp on the front of the LCI dropped.

Charlie and his company exited the LCI quickly and silently. They had taped their dog tags together and taped all loose equipment to their bodies, so there was no noise. They ran through the shallow surf and to the sandy beach. Moving quickly, they entered the town of Anzio within five minutes, unopposed, except for two German soldiers who had been shot dead on the beach.

By seven in the morning, the rangers had established a solid beachhead inside the town of Anzio, Italy.

By the end of the day, the beaches had been cleared of mines, and by the end of the following day, there were thirty-six thousand American troops and three thousand vehicles on the Anzio beachhead.

"What are you cooking?" inquired Felix as he walked up the small hillock.

"A chicken I liberated," responded Charlie.

"Smells good," commented Felix, sitting down on the ground near the fire.

"Gonna be good," agreed Charlie.

"Heard any news?" asked Felix.

"Not a word," answered Charlie. "You?"

"Nope." Felix shifted his weight. "We have been sitting here on our duffs for a week. There is no resistance. When are we going to move? We got the men and machinery. We could be in Rome by now."

"Beats me." Charlie shrugged. "I just do what I am told."

"Well, they need to tell us something soon. I talked to a guy from the 509th who was just on a patrol. He said that they went five miles and saw only three Germans," griped Felix.

"Don't know." Charlie shrugged.

At that moment, a private came running up and slid to a sitting position beside the pair.

"Are you Sergeant Morgan?" quizzed the private.

"That's right," rejoined Charlie.

"You are wanted in the captain's tent in five minutes for a briefing," explained the private.

Charlie returned from his meeting an hour and a half later. He gathered the company together for orders.

"Get the men ready. We are to make a foray toward Cisterno at midnight. Knives are the preferred weapon. We move out at midnight," explained Charlie.

The land was flat, but there were plenty of clouds covering the moon. Charlie moved the men out at midnight. They marched with the ranger stride for a half hour. Charlie could barely see the point man in front of him.

Then the point man held a hand up. Charlie stopped in his tracks and held his hand up for the man behind him. The point man ran hunched over to stop beside Charlie.

"Report," whispered Charlie.

"Eighty-eight with two machine guns just ahead," whispered Private Dan Schuster.

"Can we skirt it?" questioned Charlie.

"If we detour a hundred yards to the south, we can miss it. But—"

"We are not to engage unless we can do so quietly," instructed Charlie.

"Move south?" questioned Private Schuster.

"Yes."

The men moved out in column, detouring to the south for a hundred yards then turning east again. They entered a system of ditches and followed in one heading east. The ditch soon ended; then the land turned into moderately sized hills with large boulders.

Moving uphill silently in a small valley bordered by limestone, the group moved for three hundred yards. Charlie started getting a cold chill going down his spine, which was not the cold of the night.

Charlie could see that the valley ended in a jumble of boulders just to his front. He saw a muzzle flash from the boulders in front then heard the sound of the machine gun. The men fell on their bellies, weapons at the ready. Charlie crawled up to the side of Private Schuster.

"Did you see any sign of the enemy before the fire?" he yelled over the sound of gunfire.

Schuster did not answer. Charlie shoved Schuster's shoulder. Schuster lolled sideways, totally limp. Charlie pulled his M1 up and began firing toward the boulders. Charlie looked back and found Felix.

"Felix! Come up here and help me with Schuster," yelled Charlie.

Felix rose and ran in a crouch to where Charlie was. A grenade exploded just behind Felix, obliterating the position he had just vacated.

Felix fell down prone beside Charlie. "That was close."

"Help me get Schuster out of here. We need to retreat," commanded Charlie.

Charlie and Felix grabbed Schuster's web harness and began dragging him back. Bullets zinged off the rocks around them. They stopped and slid down beside the lead echelon.

"Withdraw by sections. One section provides cover while the other pulls back. Then the first covers while the second withdraws," commanded Charlie. "No one left behind."

The plan was executed perfectly. Bullets and grenades followed the men. The head of the valley was in sight when Charlie heard an extremely loud explosion. He felt a burning in his chest and right arm as he was thrown to the left into a large boulder. He slumped to the ground with his head spinning. He felt tired and weak. He did not want to get up or do anything except lie there.

Without Charlie on the left side of Private Schuster's body, the body fell heavily to the ground, causing Felix to fall on top of Schuster. Felix looked back and saw several muzzle flashes from the rocks to their rear. He looked over at Charlie and saw that the sergeant was still breathing. Suppressing fire came from the Americans just in front of Charlie and Felix. Felix crawled under the American fire to where Charlie was lying. Charlie was fading in and out of consciousness as Felix grabbed the left shoulder strap of his web harness in his left hand. He then grabbed the right shoulder strap of the web harness of Schuster in his right hand. Crawling, pulling, and dragging, Felix got both men—one wounded, the other dead—back to the others in the squad.

Charlie could feel himself sliding across the uneven ground on his back. The world seemed to be getting darker and darker. For some reason he could not really remember, he felt this was not correct. *It should be getting lighter, not darker*, he thought, but he wasn't sure why. Then the whole world went dark.

In the darkness, Charlie thought he heard another explosion, but he could never be sure he had actually heard it.

When Charlie awoke, he was in a large army tent with cots lined on either side. He was flat on his back and very dizzy and confused. An army nurse walked past between the rows of cots, swishing her long white dress as she walked. She was carrying a metal tray with several metal instruments on it. As she looked to the right, two of the instruments slid off the tray and clattered to the floor. Charlie was very alarmed and tried to roll to the floor and find cover. Instead, he found that his right arm was stiff and tied up to a contraption slung over the bed. His right leg was also strapped to the bars over his cot. The attempt only caused a great deal of sharp pain to shoot through his arm and leg. All he could do was groan.

Another nurse approached his bedside. In a morphine haze, he studied her face. Her black hair hung to her shoulders with curls at the ends. The bangs hung limply across her forehead contrasting against the white skin, which glistened with a light dusting of sweat. A single clump of hair caressed her left cheek, held in place with sweat. But the most striking feature of her face was her flashing blue eyes, which held unending depths.

"Nurse," croaked Charlie, "where am I?"

The nurse whirled her head toward him with a harried look. "You are on the hospital ship, *Shamrock*. You have been seriously wounded and need your rest."

"Thank you." He groaned again as he tried to shift his weight.

Though she was tired and hurried, the nurse leaned over him and asked, "Do you need some more pain medicine?"

Charlie smelled the light smell of lilac as the pain lingered. "Yes, ma'am."

"I will be back in a minute with some morphine."

The nurse strode off between the rows of bunk beds lining either side of the room. Her skirt swished back and forth as her muscular hips swayed back and forth. Charlie closed his eyes and saw her blue-eyed smile in his mind.

JIM HAWLEY

# CHAPTER 19

"IT IS SO good to have you home." Lucy beamed as she helped Charlie into the house.

"I'm very glad to be home," responded Charlie enthusiastically. "How is Coeur?"

"He's doing fine," said Lucy. She looked at Charlie with concern. "He has missed you."

"I would like to go out and see him," demanded Charlie.

"OK." Lucy looked around. "Pearl is still asleep." She took Charlie by the left arm and led him out the door. Charlie didn't use his right arm much and limped heavily on his right leg.

Coeur walked to the fence as soon as he saw Charlie. The horse placed his head over the fence and drew in a deep breath through dilated nostrils. He then exhaled with a snort. Charlie reached out with his left hand and stroked Coeur's forehead. Coeur lifted his head and turned it slightly to the left. He stared at Charlie with a flashing eye. Then the eye softened, and he returned his head to nuzzle Charlie's shoulder.

"Good boy. I will ride you soon," cooed Charlie.

Lucy sympathetically stroked Charlie's right shoulder. "Mom and Dad will be here soon to see you. They are very proud of you."

"I didn't do anything. I just did my duty," muttered Charlie. He looked at Lucy. "What about Junior? Is he still working at the Two Bar?"

Lucy looked down. "Junior joined not long after you. He was killed at Normandy."

"Oh" was Charlie's only reply. It did not seem to require any further comment. He looked at the pasture silently as a white mare pranced over to the fence.

"That is Storm. I've been riding her some. She is a real sweetheart," said Lucy with a sad smile. "Isn't she pretty?"

"She is gorgeous," replied Charlie with a thick voice. "Just like you." He looked at Lucy. "I missed you."

"I love you too, Charlie," murmured Lucy. "But the war is over now. You are on the mend. Everything is going to be OK."

"Yes, it will." Charlie looked at the warm blue June sky. Puffy small white clouds floated by in their eastward journey. "But Junior, Felix, and many others won't be part of it."

Lucy did not know how to answer, so she remained silent.

"As soon as I can ride, we need to take the horses up into the mountains. Maybe up to Esterbrook," commented Charlie without looking at her. "I missed riding." He looked down and shuffled his feet. "I rode a mule in Italy, but it wasn't the same."

"Charlie" came a booming voice from behind Charlie. "How are you feeling?"

Charlie turned and saw Carl and Erin walking across the lawn toward him.

"I am fine, sir." Charlie looked down at his slung right arm. "Well, doing well."

"Good to have you home." Carl smiled. "Lester has your job waiting for you when you get your strength back."

"Thank you, sir," replied Charlie.

"Here, Lucy, let me help Charlie back up to the yard. Your mother is in the house, waiting for you. We heard Pearl when we drove up, and she went in to get her up," said Carl, taking Charlie by the left arm.

Lucy hurried to the house, and Carl helped Charlie limp to the front of the house, where several wooden chairs sat on the lawn. Carl helped Charlie into a chair then sat in the one beside him.

"Well," began Carl, "the war's over."

"In Europe," stated Charlie. "Still going on in the Pacific. The rangers may be sent there."

"But not you?" questioned Carl.

"Not me," agreed Charlie.

"Still, it will be a good Fourth," commented Carl.

"Yep." Charlie nodded. "Hot though."

Carl leaned back in his chair. Charlie looked over at him. "Sorry to hear about Junior."

"He's buried in France," said Carl. He placed his hand over his mouth and looked up at the blue sky, which demonstrated a few puffy white clouds.

Charlie did not know what, if anything, was proper to say, so he remained silent.

Erin and Lucy were in the house, cutting the rind off the watermelon and cutting the sweet red meat into cubes.

"Another hot day," commented Erin.

"Yes, it is."

Erin looked out the kitchen window and stared at the back of the heads of the two men sitting in the wooden chairs. "How is Charlie doing?"

Lucy stopped cutting for a while and thought. "Not too bad considering. He still has nightmares. And when the wind blows the curtains at night, he tries to belly flop onto the floor." She shook her head. "It hurts him when he does that."

"I can imagine with that broken arm and metal hip," clucked Erin.

"He is nice enough and really loves Pearl, but something has changed in him," mused Lucy.

"Can't go through what he has gone through without being changed," explained Erin.

"Daddy has gained a lot of weight lately," said Lucy.

"He has been sitting around a lot," returned Erin. "Says it's too hot to do anything, but I think he just doesn't feel well." Erin washed her hands then turned back to Lucy as she was drying them. "He seems to be having some trouble with his breathing."

"He needs to see the doctor," stated Lucy.

"Good luck with that." Erin laughed.

"Well, the watermelon's ready," observed Lucy.

"Is Pearl still asleep?" asked Erin.

"Yes. But we need to wake her up soon, or she won't sleep tonight." Lucy smiled.

The two women each picked up a tray laden with cubes of cold watermelon and walked out the door.

"Well, how are you feeling, hero?" queried Erin as she walked over to the chairs.

"Not too bad, Mom," responded Charlie. "On the mend."

"Good." Erin looked around. "Another hot Fourth of July."

"Yes, ma'am," returned Charlie.

"Glad to have you home." Erin beamed.

"We have already been through that, woman," commented Carl.

"I just wanted him to know I am glad to see him home," snapped Erin.

"Thank you, ma'am." Charlie smiled.

Erin walked to Carl and lowered the tray for him to take some melon cubes. Lucy did the same for Charlie. Then the ladies took their chairs on either side of the men with the trays in their laps.

Carl looked around. "Where's Pearl?"

"She's still asleep," answered Lucy.

"Well, get her out here." Carl chuckled. "She needs to enjoy the celebration of this great nation." He looked at a red cube of melon. "And enjoy some of this wonderful watermelon."

Lucy rose, laid the tray of watermelon in Charlie's lap, and turned toward the house. "I'll get her," she said over her shoulder.

Soon, Lucy returned, leading Pearl by the hand. Pearl saw Carl and yelled, "Paw!" She ran to him and threw her little arms around him. Carl engulfed her with his large arms. Pearl looked over and grinned at Erin. She swung around in Carl's lap to face the group. She stared at Charlie without saying a word.

"She just doesn't quite know you yet, Charlie," explained Erin. "She was just born when you left and hasn't seen you for three and a half years."

Charlie dropped his head. "I know."

Lucy reached over and took Charlie's hand.

Erin leaned back in her chair. "It is nice to have the gang back for another Fourth celebration."

A breeze rustled the blue columbine flowers in the yard.

# CHAPTER 20

"ARE YOU SURE you want to spend the night up here?" questioned Lucy.

"Pearl is with your parents, the place is safe, why not?" questioned Charlie.

"Just asking," said Lucy. "But are you sure you want to spend the night?"

"Yep," affirmed Charlie.

"It's gonna be cold," stated Lucy.

"Yep," affirmed Charlie.

"Aren't you getting tired?" asked Lucy.

"Hip hurts a little, but it ain't bad," remarked Charlie.

The hooves of the horses clopped on the hardened soil as Charlie and Lucy rode Coeur and Storm up the steep slope of Sheep Mountain.

"Are we going to camp on the top?" asked Lucy.

"Nope," stated Charlie, "on the top of the next mountain over."

"I am going to be sore by the time we get back," commented Lucy.

"Don't worry, darling, you will get over it," said Charlie. "Just wait until we get there. You will love it."

They continued riding uphill. The autumn breeze cooled the people and horses. The smell of columbine and violets wafted on the air. It was warm but not hot. Flies buzzed around and Lucy occasionally had to swat at a deerfly on Storm's neck.

They reached the top of Sheep Mountain as the sun reached its zenith. Charlie dismounted and motioned for Lucy to also dismount. Lucy did so and took the reins of both horses. Charlie busied himself, starting a small fire on top of some rocks. They hobbled the horses and began heating some beans. Charlie went to Coeur and fished out some deer jerky while Lucy stirred the beans. They sat on rocks and ate while the sun beamed down on them. The view was breathtaking. To the right was Laramie Peak, rising twice as high as them. To their left and behind lay the town of Wheatland, sprawled out on the high plain.

After cleaning the dishes with sand, they repacked the horses and removed the hobbles. Mounting again, they began the trip down the western slope. They rode into the valley below then up a slope to the top of the next ridge. Just as they were approaching the top of the ridge, they saw a herd of elk off to their left. The herd continued to graze as a male raised his head and bugled.

They found an open spot on the top of the ridge and began setting up camp in the late afternoon. Charlie set up the tent then began forming a fire ring. He tied a heavy rope between two trees as a picket line. Charlie hobbled the horses to allow them to graze before being tied to the picket line. Charlie and Lucy wandered a short distance, gathering dry wood for the fire. Returning to camp, Charlie began the fire to provide warmth and cook supper.

After a simple supper, Charlie tied the horses to the picket line. They spread a blanket on the ground inside the tent then placed another blanket on top of the first. With the bed made, they went back outside the tent to the fire. The fire was small with rocks piled a foot high all the way around it. The September wind was light but cool, but the surrounding woods were very dry. Lucy brought out half a bag of marshmallows as Charlie sharpened two sticks with his pocket knife. They toasted marshmallows and basked in the fire glow as the dusk deepened into night.

"I am full," remarked Charlie.

"Me too," agreed Lucy, leaning into Charlie's shoulder. "It is beautiful up here."

Charlie looked through the fire. "Yes, it is."

"Are you tired?" asked Lucy.

"A little," Charlie admitted.

Lucy looked up at his face. It was very handsome in the light of the fire. She leaned up and kissed him with emotional ardor. She held him tightly.

"Let's go to bed," Charlie said softly. He winked at her. He stood and took Lucy by the hand, lifting her to her feet. He led her inside the tent and removed his boots. Quickly, Lucy was disrobed and under the top blanket. Charlie followed suit. Charlie enfolded her in his arms and kissed her.

"Did you see those elk?" asked Lucy.

"Yes. It is a herd I used to see here frequently. I had hoped they would still be around," answered Charlie.

"They were beautiful," commented Lucy.

"Like you," murmured Charlie.

They made love as though the world were coming to an end until late into the night.

The next morning, Charlie hobbled the horses and let them graze as he cooked bacon and fried some eggs. Lucy ate hungrily, eyeing Charlie coyly. Charlie ate quickly and quietly.

"This place reminds me a lot of the mountains of Italy," Charlie observed.

"What was it like?" inquired Lucy.

"It was beautiful and horrible," mused Charlie.

"Horrible how?" questioned Lucy.

"It was just horrible. Leave it at that," mumbled Charlie.

Charlie packed the blankets and tent as Lucy cleaned the dishes. Charlie put the fire out then packed the horses. He removed their hobbles then rechecked and poured a canteen of water on the fire. They mounted up and began the trek back home.

"I haven't heard you mention Felix since you got home. You wrote about him several times," said Lucy, making conversation. "Have you heard from him since getting home?"

"No," stated Charlie tensely. "He died in Italy." Charlie's eyes never strayed from the trail.

"Oh," said Lucy.

"Enough said about the war," ordered Charlie through gritted teeth. "Do not ask any more questions about that time."

"Yes, sir," agreed Lucy.

The horses were surefooted and made their way through the rocks without problems. They reached the peak of Sheep Mountain just after the sun reached its zenith. They ate lunch there in silence.

"I am sorry for being so sharp with you today," apologized Charlie. "I just don't want to talk or think about that time again."

"It's all right, love, I understand," answered Lucy.

"All you need to know is that it was bad," he said.

They continued riding until late afternoon when they reached Carl's berm house. Charlie held Lucy's horse as Lucy went in to get Pearl. Carl came out, holding Pearl's hand as Pearl walked beside him.

"Thank you," called out Lucy to Erin as she walked out of the house.

Carl led Pearl to the left side of Charlie's horse. He lifted her and, with Charlie's help, placed her astride the horse behind Charlie. Carl winced visibly as he lifted Pearl.

"You OK, Carl?" asked Charlie.

"Yeah. Think I pulled a muscle this morning," replied Carl, rubbing his left upper chest.

"Doing what?" questioned Charlie.

"Don't know. It is nothing," shrugged off Carl.

Charlie situated Pearl on the horse behind him and held the horse still as Lucy mounted her horse. They started off at a walk headed toward their home.

"Your dad didn't look like he felt too well," commented Charlie to Lucy.

"He is getting older," answered Lucy. "He is full of aches and pains."

"Yeah, but he looked a little peaked," observed Charlie.

Lucy thought a minute. "He did look a little under the weather."

They rode the rest of the way home in silence. Pearl remained quiet, enjoying the sway of the horse, the breeze across her cheeks, and the smell of horse sweat.

Nine months later, Lucy gave birth to their son, Michael.

# CHAPTER 21

MONDAY MORNING, CHARLIE reported to the gas station. Lester had two vehicles ready to be repaired. Charlie had been back to work for a couple of months and found that Lester had more and more work for him to do.

"Good morning, Charlie," greeted Lester.

"Good morning, sir," answered Charlie.

"Got a minute?" asked Lester.

"Sure. Just let me finish tightening this oil plug," replied Charlie.

Charlie finished then walked into Lester's office, wiping the grease from his hands.

"Hello, Charlie, have a seat," acknowledged Lester, motioning Charlie toward a wooden chair.

"Hello, Lester," returned Charlie, feeling somewhat confused. They had greeted each other just minutes before.

"Charlie, I have been thinking," said Lester, nodding. "I have been running this place for many years now."

"Yes, sir," agreed Charlie.

"And I been thinking," Lester continued. He lit a pipe then sat back in his chair. "I think it is time to take a rest."

"Yes, sir." Charlie nodded, wondering where the conversation was going.

"And I think it's time to get out of the business," said Lester, puffing on his pipe. "I will get straight to the point. How would you like to buy the place?"

Charlie's mouth fell open. "Excuse me, sir."

"This place." Lester waved his arm around. "How would you like to buy the place? You are good with customers. You're fair and are a wonderful mechanic."

"I would have to talk it over with Lucy, sir," stammered Charlie.

"Let me know soon. I will have to put it on the market if you don't buy it."

"Yes, sir," answered Charlie, standing. "Now, if you will excuse me, sir, I will get back to fixing those cars."

"That's right, son, get back to work. But think my offer over," said Lester, waving his hand.

Charlie turned back to Lester. "How much are you asking, sir?"

Lester told him, and it sounded very reasonable.

"But if you wait too long," continued Lester, "the price will go up."

"Yes, sir." Charlie left the office and went back to work on the cars. He had a difficult time the rest of the day, keeping his mind on work.

That night after supper, Charlie sat Lucy down.

"Uh-oh, this is never a good sign." Lucy giggled.

"Lucy, darling, Lester has offered to sell me the service station." Lucy looked at him openmouthed. "It is a very reasonable offer. I think that with some of my GI money and a GI loan, we can do it easily."

Lucy stared at him for a long moment. "What?"

"I said—"

"I heard what you said," Lucy cut him off, shaking her head. "I just find it hard to understand."

"You have your lunch business. I could have my own business," elucidated Charlie. "It would be great."

"I don't know how long I want to continue my business," interjected Lucy.

"That would be fine. We could rely on the station." Charlie looked down and shook his head. "I can't work horses very well anymore with this hip and arm. You could continue the restaurant or close it—whatever you want to do. But I could run the station, and we would do all right."

"Sure. I guess. If it is what you want to do, then do it," concurred Lucy.

The phone rang. Charlie walked over to the wall where the phone was mounted.

"Hello?" He listened. "When?" He listened again. "Thank you. We will be there in a minute." Charlie hung the phone up and turned to Lucy with an ashen complexion.

"Your father is at the hospital," he related, turning to Lucy. "He has had a heart attack. Get Pearl and let's go."

They drove to the hospital in silence. When they arrived, they found Erin in the waiting room, crying.

"He went to the bathroom and came out. Then he said he didn't feel so good, and just fell back. I got him here as best I could," explained Erin.

Charlie walked over to her and embraced her. "You got him here. That's what counts."

"I don't think he is doing too good," mumbled Erin. "I tried my best."

Just then the doctor came into the waiting room. "Mrs. Johansson?" Erin nodded. "Can you follow me?" The doctor led her into a modest room with a small altar and an open Bible on a pedestal. "I am sorry," began the doctor after he had closed the door, "but your husband did not make it."

"What do you mean? What are you saying?" snuffled Erin.

"I am sorry, but he is dead," said the doctor softly.

Erin sat heavily in a padded chair. "Can my children come in?" she asked through sobs.

"Certainly. I will bring them." The doctor left. In a few minutes, the door opened and Lucy came in and fell into Erin's arms. The two women cried together while Charlie stood aside and choked on the lump in his throat.

One year later, Erin joined Carl in the hereafter. The townspeople said she died of "the dwindles." Lucy always thought she died of a broken heart. The doctors, being less romantic, called it breast cancer.

# CHAPTER 22

CHARLIE WALKED IN the door and looked up as a little bell over the door tinkled.

"What you up to, Charlie?" questioned Steve Parsons, motioning Charlie over to his table.

"Just taking a lunch break," retorted Charlie. Charlie walked to the table and pulled a chair out.

"How's business?" queried Marshal Samson.

"Good," answered Charlie. "Summer rush is over, but now everybody wants cars fixed after running them hell-bent for leather all summer."

"So is Alan Burns working out for you? I hear he is a whiz of a mechanic," commented Marshal. He half turned in his chair and raised one finger. "Maria, some coffee here."

Maria Vasquez had bought the diner about fifteen years before. She strode over and poured a cup of coffee for Charlie. She was still beautiful with dark hair and eyes, but her hips had widened considerably. As she walked off, Charlie swatted her rear, allowing his hand to linger there just a little longer than was considered playful. Maria swatted at Charlie's arm, missing it by a large margin.

"You are *muy mal*," scolded Maria with a mischievous smile.

Charlie turned back to the men at the table. "Actually, he is working out very well," agreed Charlie. "He sure knows his way around an engine."

Steve Parsons was well over six feet tall and of more than ample girth. He leaned back in his chair, making Charlie wonder how long the back of the chair was going to remain intact. He was in his eighties and arthritic from years of work with cattle, fences, and horses. "How is that boy of yours doing?" he inquired. "Is he playing football this year?"

"Yeah, he's playing fullback," Charlie explained. "He's actually doing pretty good for a sophomore."

"Not that you are biased or nothin'," commented Marshal. Marshal Samson was a middle-aged bachelor who worked as a ranch foreman.

He was five feet nine inches tall and thin. His skin was tanned and leathery and was usually found with a self-rolled cigarette hanging out of his mouth.

"I am biased, and I make no bones about it." Charlie grinned.

"Where is that pretty little gal, Pearl?" questioned Marshal.

"She is a freshman at UCLA," expounded Charlie. "She is studying political science."

"What is that?" questioned Steve.

"I don't know. Politics or something like that," replied Charlie. "Actually, I don't know how much studying she is doing."

"Studying the boys, I imagine." Marshal laughed, looking at Steve then Charlie.

"Yeah," said Charlie, shaking his head. "She is pretty excited. I can't wait until she gets home at Christmas."

"Isn't she gonna come home for Thanksgiving?" asked Steve.

"I doubt it," grunted Charlie. "I can't afford it for Thanksgiving and Christmas."

"Do you gentlemen want anything to eat?" questioned Maria, walking up with a pot of coffee.

"Nothing for me, thanks. Just freshen the coffee," answered Marshal.

"What is the special for the day?" asked Charlie.

"I call it the Lucy sandwich. It is roast beef on homemade bread, with mashed potatoes," replied Maria.

"I'll have that," ordered Charlie.

"And for you?" asked Maria, turning to Steve.

"I'll have the same."

"Two specials coming up." Maria smiled as she poured coffee for all three.

Charlie watched Maria saunter off. His mouth watered as he watched her long dark hair sway as she walked.

Marshal watched Charlie's face as Maria walked off. When she went into the back kitchen, Marshal questioned Charlie. "You two have something going on?"

Charlie's eyes snapped back to Marshal. A fleeting dark look passed his face. "Of course not," denied Charlie.

Steve and Marshal looked at each other and grinned.

"So," started Steve, leaning back, "what do you fellas think of that Cuban crap?"

"Kennedy sure screwed that one up," commented Charlie.

"What did he screw up?" queried Marshal. Marshal was a cowboy and did not keep up with politics.

"The Bay of Pigs fiasco," explained Charlie. Charlie looked at Marshal and noted the blank look on his face. "Kennedy sent some men and Cuban immigrants to Cuba to overthrow Castro."

Marshal looked back and forth from Steve to Charlie. "He did?"

"Yeah," grunted Steve.

"How did it go?" wondered Marshal.

"Not well," replied Charlie, laughing. Steve chuckled.

"So what's going on now?" asked Marshal.

"Don't your kids go to school?" questioned Charlie.

"Yes, why?" responded Marshal.

"Haven't they told you about hiding under their desks, preparing for nuclear war?" wondered Charlie.

"Yeah. But they have been doing that for a while now," Marshal said, puzzled.

"So they will be doing it more now," explained Charlie. "The Russians are setting up a missile site in Cuba now."

"They are? Why?"

Steve turned in his chair to face Marshal. "To bomb us. Why do you think?"

Maria arrived with their food and placed the steaming plates in front of them. Her hand lingered just slightly longer when putting Charlie's plate in front of him.

The men ate in silence and paid their bills and left.

Charlie left work an hour early and let Alan close up the station. He drove down the alley behind the diner. He looked around as he got out of the truck. He went into the store through the back door.

Thirty minutes later, Charlie left the back door with a cup of coffee in his hands. He got in his truck and drove off.

# CHAPTER 23

"COME ON, MICHAEL, you need to eat some meat before the game," expounded Charlie.

"Yes, sir. But I'm not hungry," countered Michael. Michael had grown into a muscular five-foot-eleven-inch sixteen-year-old. He was ending his sophomore football season at the state championship game. They were to play Douglas tonight, and he was a little nervous.

"Now, hit your speed fast and don't slow down looking for a hole in the line. Keep the steam up and plow through," ordered Charlie. "Don't be afraid of those boys. They are as scared as you are."

"I know, Dad. And I'm not scared," countered Michael, rubbing his hand through his crew cut hair.

"Anyway, eat your roast beef," commanded Charlie.

The game started, and Charlie made his way into the stand. He had a Coke in one hand and two hot dogs in the other. His belly now hung over his belt, making his jacket zipper strain over his middle. He walked in front of the wooden seats until he found an area that would give him enough space to sit without being crowded.

"Come on, Michael, drop your shoulders," he roared as Michael ran onto the field.

Lucy sat beside him but not too close. Charlie was now a preponderant eater and not very dainty, so she did not sit too close in order not to suffer from flailing elbows and mustard stains.

"Hit somebody, Michael!" Charlie screamed as the first play wound down. He turned to Lucy. "Did you see him tiptoe up into the line like a girl?"

"Don't be so hard on him," scolded Lucy.

"He needs to just play football or become a cheerleader," snapped Charlie.

The first half continued, and at the half, the score was Wheatland, 14; Douglas, 21. When the buzzer sounded to end the half, Charlie rose, hitched up his pants, and turned to Lucy. "I am going to the truck for a minute."

"What for?" inquired Lucy.

"A cigarette," answered Charlie as he moved off down the bleachers.

Charlie went out to the parking lot and sauntered to his truck. He opened the door and removed a pack of Lucky Strike from the dashboard. He thumped a cigarette from the pack and stuck it in his mouth. He lit the cigarette then looked around. Seeing no one, he leaned back into the truck, replaced the lighter, and reached into the glove compartment. He removed a small bottle then stood up. He looked around again then took a long drink from the bottle.

When he returned to the bleachers, he sat down heavily beside Lucy.

"I had to have a cigarette," he commented.

Lucy smelled the whiskey breath and rolled her eyes.

"Has the third quarter started?" asked Charlie.

"Just started," grunted Lucy.

The Wheatland boys took the kickoff and ran it back from their thirty-yard line to the forty-five. The offense came onto the field, and Michael was fullback. The ball was snapped, and the handoff went to Michael. He lowered his shoulders and ran through the line. Then, five yards down the line, he met the linebacker. He was upended and landed on his back. He heard and felt a loud crack from his right arm. His arm hurt so much, he was unable to rise. The coaches ran to the field along with the trainer, who was a high school senior.

"Get up, Michael. Don't lay there like a girl!" shouted Charlie. He sat back down and turned to Lucy. "He is such a girl."

"He's hurt," chastised Lucy.

"He's a baby. You baby him too much," accused Charlie.

Without another word, Charlie rose and walked down the bleachers and onto the sidelines, where Michael was being helped.

"What are you doing?" demanded Charlie.

"He's hurt," said Coach Turner, stepping between the two. "He needs to be evaluated by a doctor."

"He needs to get tough and get back into the game," admonished Charlie.

"He can't go back in until he is evaluated by a doctor. The ambulance crew will take him to the hospital," explained Coach Turner.

"I can take him," grunted Charlie.

"OK, but take him right there," stated Coach Turner, puffing his chest out.

Charlie ran his hand through his thinning hair. "OK."

Charlie walked to the bottom of the bleachers, leading Michael by the left arm and motioned for Lucy to go to him. He took Lucy in the truck and headed toward the hospital. Lucy knew better than to ask questions though she was worried about Michael.

They drove in the old truck to the hospital, and Charlie helped Michael into the lobby.

"I got a kid here with a hurt arm," slurred Charlie.

"Yes," answered the nurse, "we got a call from the doctor. He was at the game and will be here shortly."

Just then the door opened, and a tall young man in a white shirt, a tie, and a heavy coat entered.

"This way, folks," ordered Dr. Howshar. He led them down a short hall to a well-lit large room. "Have a seat over on that bed," stated Dr. Howshar, indicating a gurney in the middle of the room.

Charlie led Michael to the gurney and clumsily helped him sit. Dr. Howshar walked over and pushed on Michael's forearm. He hummed as he pushed and prodded. Then he looked up. "This arm is broken. I need to get an x-ray."

The x-ray was done, and it took five minutes to develop the pictures. Dr. Howshar held the black-and-clear celluloid up toward the light as he walked to the x-ray view box hung on the wall at the side of the room. He flicked the film up, trapping it under the clamp. He pointed. "There it is."

Charlie looked but could not really tell anything. His vision was a little bleary. "Yep."

"You gotta keep this arm elevated. Otherwise, it will swell and make the cast too tight," explained Dr. Howshar. "Put a cold pack on it four times a day." Dr. Howshar explained this and other things as he placed a cast on Michael's forearm.

Dr. Howshar turned to Charlie. "I was at the game. The boy is a good player, but it is just a game."

"But—" began Charlie.

"No buts. It *is* a game. Now the boy played well. Go a little easier on him," admonished the doctor.

Charlie looked from the doctor to Michael and back to the doctor. "Yeah, OK, Doc."

They left the hospital with Charlie in the lead, mumbling under his breath. Lucy followed with a hand on Michael's left arm. The right arm was in a sling.

"Championship game," grumbled Charlie, "and he gotta 'hurt' his little arm."

"I tried, Dad," exclaimed Michael.

"Oh, get in the truck," ordered Charlie.

"The game is over," stated Lucy. "And the season is over. There will be another season."

"Get in the truck," repeated Charlie.

The next week was difficult for Michael as his arm hurt and he had a difficult time in school trying to write.

That Friday morning, Michael went to school and found his seat in his homeroom. The day was typical. English class, where he did well but was continually bored, was his second class. Then algebra class was third period. It was down the hall. He liked algebra much better than he liked any of his other classes. It seemed to make sense.

The bell rang, and he gathered up his books as best he could and walked to his locker. He opened the locker and put his books in. Then he took out his library book and turned to head toward study hall. He remembered he had some algebra homework, so he took out his algebra book as well. He closed the door of the locker and turned toward the study hall. The turn brought him face-to-face with Kathy Campbell. She was tall with long blond hair and bright blue eyes.

"Hello," greeted Kathy.

"Hi," returned Michael. He ducked his head and scooted around her and hurried to study hall. He had had a crush on Kathy for two years, but so had the rest of the school. Finding the courage to talk to her was something he had never been able to do.

He made it to study hall and got into his seat just as the bell rang.

"Well, I am glad to see you decided to join us," commented Mr. Turner sarcastically. He looked around the room. "Answer your name as I call roll." With that, he called out the names of all the students scheduled for class at that time. Every one of the students answered, meaning no one was absent. "Get to work. I am sure you have something to keep yourselves busy."

Michael opened his algebra and, with some difficulty, turned the pages to the current assignment. The math itself was not difficult, but the writing of the problem and showing his work left-handedly seemed to take forever. He had worked for what seemed a long time when the intercom clicked, indicating an announcement was imminent. Seconds later, the announcement came.

"Attention, attention. It has just been announced that President Kennedy has been shot," came the voice of Mr. Jackson. "Your parents are being notified, and school will be dismissed. Buses will be running as usual. Please gather your belongings and prepare to load buses."

Michael was stunned. He was not too interested in politics—but who would kill the president and why?

Lucy arrived at the school in fifteen minutes and walked to Michael's study hall.

"Go ahead and get your books," Lucy told Michael as he walked out of the class.

Michael walked from the class and trudged to his locker. He opened the locker and added his American literature book to his stack. He closed the locker door and turned to face Kathy again. She was tall and beautiful with tears streaming down her cheeks, which made her even more beautiful. She stepped forward and enfolded Michael in her arms. He pressed his face against her shoulder and smelled her perfume. The embrace hurt his arm, but he paid no attention to that.

"Isn't it horrible?" cried Kathy.

"Terrible," answered Michael, giving her neck a little kiss.

# CHAPTER 24

"YOU JUST GRADUATED high school. You can't join the army," enjoined Charlie. "You have to go to college first."

"I'm ready for the army. I am in the best shape of my life. Now is the time," returned Michael defiantly.

"You need my permission to join." Charlie smirked.

"No, I don't. I have registered for the draft, and it's just a matter of time before they'll draw my name. I might as well join up now," countered Michael.

Charlie was stumped. He stared at Michael for a full minute then turned and walked off. As he stomped out the door, he passed Lucy. "See if you can talk some sense into him."

*Nobody could stop you when you left me and a baby to fight a war,* thought Lucy.

Michael walked up to Lucy. "Don't you see, Mom, if I join, I have a better chance of being assigned stateside? Most of the draftees are going to Vietnam. I would rather join," pleaded Michael.

Lucy shook her head as she dried the lunch dishes. She shrugged her shoulders and used her right upper arm to wipe the tear rolling down her right cheek.

Without another word, Michael stomped out the door and got into his yellow VW Bug. He started the engine and spun out of the dirt driveway, spewing July dust behind him. Ten minutes later, he was at Josh Behr's house. Josh was his best friend since they were freshmen.

A few minutes later, Charlie returned.

"Did he leave?" quizzed Charlie.

"Yes. I think he is going to join up," answered Lucy.

"Damn fool. He is such a hothead idiot," roared Charlie.

"Yes, he's just like his father," responded Lucy with her hands on her hips.

Charlie looked down then looked back up at Lucy with a tear in his eye. "Coeur is down. I am afraid he will not be getting back up."

"Come on, Josh, go to Cheyenne with me and join up," entreated Michael.

"I can't. I have been accepted at Colorado State. I am going to go to medical school," replied Josh.

Michael looked down and kicked at the dirt in the driveway. "At least go with me to Cheyenne so I can sign up."

Josh looked around. "OK. Let me tell my folks."

"Make it fast."

A month later, Michael was doing his basic training at Fort Sill, Oklahoma.

"What do you think you are doing?" screamed Master Sergeant Stevens.

Michael stood at attention. "Disposing of a cigarette, Sergeant," answered Michael loudly.

"You do not leave dead comrades on the field without proper attention," shouted Sergeant Stevens. "That soldier deserves better than just being thrown on the ground. Take that soldier up and dispose of the body properly." The sergeant was nose to nose with Michael.

"Yes, Sergeant," yelled Michael. Michael bent down and picked up the cigarette butt.

"Now fieldstrip that soldier," bawled the sergeant.

Michael peeled the paper from the tobacco and spread the tobacco to the wind. He still held the paper and the filter.

"Now bury that soldier," spat the sergeant.

Michael bent down and dug a shallow hole in the dirt. He placed the filter and the paper in the hole and covered it over with the dirt.

"Do you know what you just did?" questioned Sergeant Stevens.

"Yes, sir," answered Michael. "I buried a comrade."

"No, you buried your comrade incorrectly," shouted the sergeant. Michael stared straight ahead. "You buried that soldier with his head facing north. It should be facing east."

Michael kneeled again and dug up the filter. He turned it ninety degrees and reburied it.

"That is better, Private. When you are far from home, remember this lesson. Bury any dead comrades and bring still-living ones back," lectured the sergeant. "And bury your dead with their heads toward home."

"Yes, Sergeant. Thank you, Sergeant," snapped Michael as he stood at attention.

"Now go wash yourself up and remember to always fieldstrip your butts," returned the sergeant.

# CHAPTER 25

"**I** NEED A tunnel rat up here," yelled Lieutenant Carlisle, pointing to a small hole in the ground.

"Here, sir," yelled Corporal Markham, trotting up. The corporal dropped his pack, laid his M16 against it, and removed his helmet. He pulled his cap from the pack and placed it on so that the bill pointed backward. "In I go." He looked around. "Alice in Wonderland," he stated as he slipped headfirst into the hole.

"OK, relax. This may take a while," commanded the lieutenant. "Smoke 'em if you got 'em."

Michael found a place in the foliage where he could sit down. He leaned back so that the forty-pound pack rested on the ground. He took out a pack of cigarettes and tapped one out. He stuck it between dry, cracking lips and lit it. He leaned his head back and looked at the sunlight streaming through the palms. In a different time—a different place—it would have been really beautiful.

Thirty minutes later, the tunnel rat returned. He crawled out and threw four human ears on the ground. "I also got this," he commented, handing the lieutenant a stack of papers.

"That man is boocoo dinky dau," commented Washington.

Isaac Leroy Washington was a six-foot-three-inch-tall black man from Detroit. He was a short-timer.

Michael nodded at Washington then his head jerked forward as he heard a zip pop, like large raindrops hitting the foliage. The large elephant-ear leaves waved as bullets passed through them. Michael pulled his M16 up as he rolled to the prone position in one fluid motion.

"Shit—shit! Where did that come from?" yelled Washington.

"Shut up!" retorted Sergeant Morris.

Now everybody was prone. Sergeant Morris crawled up to Lieutenant Carlisle. "They're just ahead, sir . . . in the foliage."

"Take three men and flank them. I will lay down covering fire," ordered the lieutenant. "Whistle when you are ready to move."

Sergeant Morris grabbed two men and motioned them to follow him. Then he grabbed Washington by the web suspenders and motioned him to follow.

"Why I gotta go, Sarge? I only got twenty-one days and a wake-up, and I am on that freedom bird," complained Washington.

"Shut up and follow me," whispered the sergeant through gritted teeth. The sergeant then gave a low bird whistle and motioned the three others to follow him.

Michael moved up until he was in a line with Lieutenant Carlisle and the others of the platoon. Carlisle raised a hand just above his shoulder. He hesitated a minute then brought the hand down. Michael and the rest of the platoon began firing into the foliage in front of them. The noise was deafening as the foliage shattered and flew about in green chunks. The volley lasted for almost a minute then began to slow down. Before the men stopped firing altogether, some shooting was heard to their front and right.

When the firing to their front slowed down, Lieutenant Carlisle lifted his hand again and brought it forward. The men rose to a crouch and began moving forward. Michael heard a groan to his left and looked over to see a wounded NVA soldier raise his AK-47. Tex Millican, to Michael's left, shot the NVA point-blank, and the threat was averted.

"Good shootin', Tex," whispered Michael.

"Sergeant," yelled Lieutenant Carlisle, "assemble the platoon."

Soon they were on the march again. They finished the circular patrol without further incident.

After reaching the forward base and being dismissed, Michael put his pack in his hooch and slung his M16 over his right shoulder and went to the latrine.

He returned to the mound of dirt outside his hooch and sat down, lighting up a cigarette. He thoughtfully puffed smoke as he scanned the tree line outside the kill zone.

"They gonna have steak tonight," said Tex, sitting down beside him.

"Sounds good," answered Michael. Then he thought about it. "What kind of steak?"

"Don't matter—beef steak, buffalo steak, water buffalo steak—all same, same." Tex shrugged.

Michael looked at him. "Water buffalo tastes like combat boots."

"Still same, same." Tex grinned.

"Did we lose any today?" questioned Michael.

"Naw. Gooks lost twenty, though," answered Tex.

"Nice body count." Michael nodded.

"Yep," agreed Tex. Tex slugged Michael in the shoulder. "Come on, let's go get some steak."

The steaks were good—*probably* beef steak—and the beer was warm. The beer was always warm.

The next morning, Michael walked out of his underground hooch and walked toward the latrine. He had only taken about three steps when he heard whistles and bugles blaring from the jungle just past the cleared kill zone. He ran to his post with his M16 at the ready. Within seconds, the kill zone was full of running, screaming short Asians with rounded pith helmets.

Michael took aim and pulled the trigger. He saw the NVA soldier throw his arms up and fall backward. After that, he aimed, fired, then shifted the aim without waiting to see if the round connected.

"Shit, they're almost to the wire!" Michael heard someone yell.

Then he saw a thin trail of white smoke leave the jungle, snaking its way toward the fortifications.

"Incoming!" and "RPGs!" he heard several people yell almost simultaneously. He ducked as the trail of smoke streaked over his head. Then he looked back up over the earthworks and began firing again.

"Angels on our shoulders!" yelled Tex, who was lying against the earthworks beside Michael.

Michael looked at Tex. He hadn't realized his friend was there. Tex grinned and pointed up.

Michael looked up and saw a flight of four F-4 Phantoms coming in low and fast. Within seconds, the tree line was engulfed in a flood of fire. It rolled out onto the NVA soldiers who had just entered the kill zone.

"Crispy critters" came Washington's voice from the other side of Tex.

"Snake and nape," commented Tex.

Michael nodded.

"How long you got?" questioned Tex making nervous conversation.

Michael looked at him. "Eighty-five and a wake-up."

"Sixty-two here," grunted Tex. "Think they'll come back?"

"They always do," replied Michael, nodding.

Thirty minutes later, the trumpets blared again. The NVA came out of the jungle en masse.

"Where's the cavalry when you need them?" asked Michael.

"They'll be here," replied Tex.

Michael fired until his clip was empty, then he reloaded.

He saw the RPG smoke from the tree line and watched the trail as it writhed right at him. He slipped down behind the dirt barrier and prayed with his face against the dank, moist dirt. The RPG passed just over his head and exploded in the dust behind him. "Thank you, God," he said softly.

Soon the sound of jets, machine-gun fire, and exploding bombs revived Michael's courage. He looked over the berm and saw the carnage as the air force drove the NVA back once again.

"Think they'll come back?" queried Michael.

"Maybe," answered Tex.

But they did not come back.

# CHAPTER 26

"LIEUTENANT WANTS TO see you," stated Tex, jerking his thumb back toward the command post.

"What for?" quizzed Michael.

"They don't tell me diddly," replied Tex.

Michael hoisted his M16 and trotted over to the command post. He ducked under the low beam as he walked in. "You sent for me, sir?"

"Yes, Morgan, take a seat," said Lieutenant Carlisle, indicating a chair on the other side of his desk. "It has been a month since the attack here, and we haven't seen or heard shit of the enemy."

"Yes, sir," replied Michael.

"I don't think we will be targeted for a while. So here is a list of supplies we need from Saigon," explained the lieutenant, pushing a piece of paper across the desk toward Michael. "There is a chopper leaving here in twenty minutes. Be on it. Get the supplies and meet the chopper tomorrow at the same time." He looked closely at Michael. "Do you understand, Corporal Morgan?"

"Yes, sir." Michael nodded.

"Then *di-di*. Get out of my sight."

Michael hurried to his hooch and changed into his cleanest uniform. It was clean but a little faded. Still, it would have to work. He caught the chopper and, in a short time, was in Saigon.

Michael made his way from the landing zone to the supply depot and showed the supply sergeant his list. The sergeant took the list and studied it. The sergeant looked up at Michael and said, "Folks in hell wanting ice water."

"Yes, Sergeant. When I get promoted and move up to hell, I will remember that."

"Very funny, Corporal. I will have this for you in two days."

"No, Sergeant, I have to leave with it tomorrow."

The sergeant glared at Michael. "All right. You grunts think you run this war. Now get out of my shop!"

Michael did an about-face and left quickly. This was not his first time in Saigon, so he felt no need for sightseeing. He went to a bar he had visited before. There were Vietnamese women there in various stages of undress, and the beer was usually relatively cold.

He ordered a beer as Nancy Sinatra belted "These Boots Are Made for Walking" from an old jukebox.

"You wanna fucky fucky or sucky sucky?" asked a prostitute about four and a half feet tall.

"I want a beer," grunted Michael.

"I love you long time. You come with me," cooed the prostitute.

He shouldered past her and went to the bar, where he got his beer. He sat on a stool and grinned as he watched a Betty Crocker soldier negotiate a price with the short prostitute and be led into a back room. He chuckled as he raised his beer. These Betty Crockers with their pressed uniforms and gold braids were such a joke. He finished the beer and slid some paper money over to the barkeep. Then he turned and walked into the street. He looked right and left, trying to decide what his next move should be. Then the building behind him exploded. He was thrown forward to the street, with black smoke rolling over and past him. Glass tinkled as it skittered across the pavement.

Michael looked left and right. He felt warm blood trickle down his left cheek. He pushed himself up with his arms and tried to rise, but his legs did not obey. He lowered himself back to the pavement and breathed heavily as he heard the ambulance sirens coming his way.

He remembered waking up in the hospital and hearing a beautiful, dark-haired nurse tell him he had the "million-dollar wound." He never remembered much about Vietnam after that.

# CHAPTER 27

I T WAS A warm indian summer day in October. Daylight savings time had not kicked in yet, so it was still late when it got dark. I finished making evening rounds about seven o'clock and decided to stop by the Wheatland Inn for supper. I walked in and was greeted by Jennifer Wilson.

"We ain't too busy right now, so sit where you want," she greeted.

"Thank you," I replied.

"Hey, Doc," came a cry from the corner booth.

"Hey, Tony," I replied with a slight wave.

"Come join us," invited Tony. Tony was a local rancher, about six feet three inches tall. He was in his early seventies and had ranched here all his life. He had a spread to the east of town.

I walked over and sat beside Tony. A man in his mid to late fifties sat across the table.

"This here's Mark Bronson," stated Tony, indicating the man across the table.

I half stood and reached across the table and shook hands with Mark. I sat back down.

"What would you like to drink?" asked Jennifer, standing over the table.

"Iced tea, please," I replied.

"Lemon?" she quizzed.

"Yes, thank you," I answered. She turned to walk off. "And a chicken fried steak."

Jennifer turned around. "Large or small?"

"Small," I replied. "With white gravy, please."

Jennifer turned and walked back to the kitchen, scribbling on her order pad.

I looked over at Mark Bronson. "You rent Lucy Morgan's pasture, don't you?"

"Yep." He looked around. "Have you seen her lately?"

"No, no, she hasn't been in for a while," I replied cautiously.

"I don't think she is doing so good," commented Mark.

"Why do you say that?" I questioned.

"Well, she takes good care of that old dog, but she keeps ordering hay," Mark stated.

I nodded my head. "Yep, for her horses."

"She ain't had no horses out there since her husband died," explained Mark, shaking his head. "And the other day, I went to pay the pasture rent, and she said the 'little people' were keeping her awake all night."

"Little people?" I questioned.

"Yep. Says there are 'little people' living in her attic. They keep talking and bothering her," replied Mark.

"Maybe she has some skeletons in the closet too." Tony chuckled.

I turned to Tony. "What kind of skeletons?"

"Well, her husband was killed in a car wreck many years ago," Tony remarked.

"Yeah, he was pulling a trailer to pick up a horse in Fort Collins and missed a curve," reflected Mark. "He and the Mexican woman riding with him were killed immediately. Always had some questions about that."

I looked from Mark to Tony and back to Mark. "They have any kids—Mr. Morgan and Lucy?"

"They had a girl," expounded Tony. "She went to school in California and got mixed up with a wrong crowd. Died from a drug overdose in the early seventies."

"Had a son," continued Mark. "He went to Vietnam and came home confined to a wheelchair. He and his father got into an argument, and he moved to California just before the old man died."

Mark and Tony sipped their coffee as Jennifer brought my chicken fried steak with mashed potatoes.

"Is he still alive—the boy?" I asked between bites of the steak.

"Far as I know," answered Mark. "Last I heard he was in a small town in California, doing some kind of computer work."

"Yep, doing computer programs for the government as I recall," agreed Tony.

"Hmm," I mumbled through a mouthful of potatoes. I swallowed the mouthful. "I was out at her place one evening last winter to feed her dog, and I saw a horse there."

"Was it getting dark?" queried Mark.

"Yes, it was pretty dark," I replied.

"It was just the light playing tricks on you. Ain't no horses around there." Mark chuckled. He took a sip of coffee. "You got any rain out your way?" questioned Mark, looking at Tony.

"Dry as a bone," replied Tony.

The conversation about the weather, the price of cattle, and other things of local interest continued until they had finished their coffee.

Jennifer came up and asked if I wanted anything else. I said no and told her to give me the ticket for all three of us. Mark and Tony made a mild protest then thanked me and finished their coffee.

Mark stood. "You really should have a look at Lucy."

"I will," I assured him.

# CHAPTER 28

I T WAS A week later before I saw Lucy. She was brought to the office by Marion Nelson. Marion is a forty-something-year-old woman who lives relatively close to Lucy. In Wyoming terms, that is within five miles. I gathered, after talking to them for only a few minutes, that Lucy's mental state had drastically deteriorated. Her early memories appeared to be intact, and most of the midterm memories were all right. But everything since 1980 was jumbled, corrupted, or just plain missing.

Her legs were swollen like tree trunks, and her lungs were full of fluid, but she had no fever.

"Lucy, you need to go back into the hospital for a day or two," I told her without leaving room for argument.

"Yes, sir."

I admitted Lucy and treated her congestive heart failure. I wrote for a psychological consult, and my fears were confirmed—Lucy was suffering from Alzheimer's disease.

"Lucy," I began as I rounded on her the second hospital day, "you need to move in to the nursing home."

"What?" she questioned.

"The nursing home. There will be others there who are about your age and people to help you."

"The nursing home?" she repeated.

"Yes."

"OK," she agreed.

I had expected more of a fight. I did not think she would agree so easily.

"What about Panda?" she inquired.

"I will take him and get him cleaned up. Then I will bring him to see you from time to time," I offered. The nurse gave me a strange look. I looked at her. "If the vet clears her, she can visit in the nursing home." The nurse nodded.

"That sounds fine, Doctor," agreed Lucy.

"Lucy," I began.

"Yes, Doctor." Lucy nodded.

"Do you know where your son is living now?" I inquired, smiling.

"In Redwood, California." She smiled.

"Thank you," I replied. I wrote in her chart then left the room.

The next day, Lucy was stationed in her own room in the nursing home. She knew many of the people there—many of whom she had served dinner on Thanksgiving.

After making nursing home rounds and dictating Lucy's admission history and physical, I left for lunch. Before going to lunch, I stopped by the sheriff's office. I knew the sheriff as I had seen him in the clinic several times.

"What can I do for you, Doc?" asked the sheriff.

"I am looking for someone," I began.

"Who?" inquired the sheriff.

"Michael Carl Morgan," I replied.

"Lucy's boy?" questioned the sheriff. "Why?"

"Lucy is in the nursing home, and I am afraid she will not do well. As far as I know, Michael is her only living relative. I would like to get in touch with him—for her," I explained.

"Give me a few days." The sheriff nodded.

True to his word, two days later, the sheriff showed up at my office with Michael's address, phone number, and e-mail address. He was living in Redwood, California, and doing well in the computer business.

I tried calling him several times that day but got no answer. That evening, I sent him an e-mail without much hope of getting a reply. The next day, however, I received an e-mail from him, which gave a different phone number.

The next day, I called the number on the e-mail.

"Good morning, Two Gig Computer Specialists, how may I help you?" came the voice on the other end of the phone.

"Yes, is Michael Morgan there?" I asked.

"Just a moment, please," returned the voice.

Calming classical music came over the phone, then a click, then a deep male voice. "This is Michael Morgan."

"Mr. Morgan, my name is Dr. Jim Holland. I am your mother's doctor."

A long pause. "How can I help you?"

"Well, I just wanted to let you know that your mother is in the nursing home and not doing well," I announced.

"In what way 'not doing well'?" questioned Michael.

"Well, she is very ill. She has congestive heart failure and Alzheimer's disease," I paused. "I feel it would be good if you came out here to arrange disposition of the ranch and get things in order."

"I see," returned Michael. "I am rather busy right now. Perhaps around Christmas I could make it out there."

"Your mother is in serious condition. It would be better if you could make it by Thanksgiving," I countered.

"I will be out there around Christmas" came the answer. The phone went dead.

Two days before Thanksgiving, I trudged through the snow from my office to the hospital.

My first patient was Mrs. Hoff. Mrs. Hoff was five feet nothing and close to three hundred pounds. She had smoked one to two packs of cigarettes a day for thirty years and had quit smoking last year when she was in the hospital. Since then she had actually declined, the damage already having been done. She was in the hospital this time with a major right lower-lobe pneumonia. I looked at her chart and noted that we needed to give her lots of oxygen to keep her blood oxygen saturation in an acceptable range. She had been on IV antibiotics for two days and was not really improving. I changed antibiotics even though the cultures were not back yet.

The only other patient I had was Shirley Campbell. She was twenty years old with pyelonephritis and was responding well to the antibiotics. Another day of IVs, and she would be going home.

It didn't take long to see these two, so I went over to the nursing home to make my monthly rounds.

I saved Lucy for last, and when I finally entered her room, she looked at me with a bright smile. "Hello, Doctor."

"Hello, Lucy. How are you feeling today?"

"I feel like running a race." She beamed.

"Well, let's wait a while before taking off." I laughed. I glanced at her chart then closed it and looked at her. "Want some coffee?"

"Got some. Do you want me to get you some?" she offered.

"I'll get it and be right back," I responded. I walked three doors down to the coffee machine and poured myself a cup then returned to her room.

"Hello, Doctor." Lucy beamed.

"Hello, Lucy." I nodded. "How are you feeling?" I took a sip of coffee and awaited the answer.

"Not so good," she replied.

I glanced at her lower legs, which were bare and looked like elephant legs. "You don't have your compression stockings on," I commented.

"I don't like them. They hurt," she complained.

"But you gotta wear them. It will help your heart," I admonished.

"Putting those things on my legs will help my heart?" she questioned disbelievingly.

"Yep," I replied. "And you need to put them up—like on a footstool."

"Sure, honey, I can do that." She smiled.

I pushed the footstool up in front of her chair, but she made no effort to raise her legs. I lifted her legs by the ankles and pushed the footstool under with my foot.

"Is Michael coming today?" she questioned.

I wondered where that came from. I had not told her or anyone else that I had found and contacted Michael.

"Is that bastard Charlie coming?" she snorted. "Where the hell is he?"

"Charlie is not coming," I said. "He died a long time ago."

"Oh yeah." She flapped her hand toward me. "I knew that."

She leaned forward and coughed mightily.

"You know, I got something I gotta tell you," she wheezed.

"OK. I'm listening," I replied, leaning forward.

She caught her breath and stared at me with deep blue eyes. "Do you want some coffee?"

"I've got some, thank you," I answered.

She stared at me for a long minute. "Glad you stopped by."

"You rest some," I admonished. "And keep those legs elevated."

I returned to the nurse's station to dictate the monthly note. I wrote an order to increase her Lasix and lectured the nurse about keeping her antiembolism stockings on.

# CHAPTER 29

CHRISTMAS EVE MORNING, I opened the office and saw patients only until noon. It was a light morning, and I mainly used the time to catch up on paperwork—which is now all done on the computer, so it was computer work.

Around eleven thirty, I got a call from the nursing home that Lucy was not doing well. Her breathing was very labored.

I shut off the computer and headed to the nursing home. Lucy was weak and unable to rise. She could barely lift her arms. Her breathing was fast and shallow.

"Hello, Doc," croaked Lucy.

"Save your breath, Lucy," I ordered.

"I gotta tell you something," she whispered so low that I had to move closer to hear her.

"Hush, now," I replied. I turned to the nurse. "She needs an IV now."

"We don't do that here," replied the nurse.

"Get the IV now. Then we can move her to the hospital," I commanded a little too loudly.

"Yes, sir," she responded as she left the room to get the IV tray.

"I cut the brake line," whispered Lucy.

"What?" I responded, a little confused.

"I knew he was taking that harlot with him, so I cut the brake line." She grinned.

"Hush now. Save your breath," I countered.

"I had helped him work on that truck before. I knew how to find the brake line and cut it," Lucy said through dry lips. "Did you see the horse?"

"There are no horses left out there," I replied.

"Sure there is a black stallion out there." Lucy nodded. "That is Coeur."

"Cur?" I questioned.

"No, Coeur—pronounced like *coor*. It is French," Lucy explained. "Charlie named him. Said it is French for *heart*. He is still out there."

"Save your breath," I commanded again.

"I cut the brake lines," whispered Lucy, nodding. And Lucy smiled. But it wasn't a pleasant smile. It was almost an evil smile.

The nurse returned with the IV kit.

"Get an IV started and give forty milligrams of Lasix, then get her to the hospital," I snapped.

I immediately wrote the order to directly admit her to the hospital. I walked through the tunnel to the hospital and sat down in the doctor's dictation room and began writing orders on a sheet of paper. Our hospital uses the computer for all orders and notes, but she was not entered into the system yet, so I could not put them in the computer. I find it easier to write the orders first then put them in the computer anyway.

By the time they got her to a room and registered, I had in mind what she needed. Her heart rate had become irregular and her breathing was shallow. Her chest x-ray did not show pneumonia, but it did show significant failure. She responded only to physical stimulation.

After my initial exam of Lucy, I made a call to Michael. After my first conversation with him, he had given me his cell phone number, so I was sure of talking to him.

"Hello" came Michael's voice.

"Michael? Where are you?" I asked.

"I am in, just passing through Rock Springs. I will be there in about six hours," answered Michael.

"Your mother is not doing well. I have her in the hospital now," I stated. I hesitated. "She may not last six hours."

"I will get there as soon as I can," responded Michael.

I hung up the phone and continued writing orders. When I had finished, I walked to Lucy's room. I looked at the cardiac monitor and saw that her heart rate was slowing.

"Give her a milligram of atropine," I ordered. The nurse left the room. In less than a minute, she returned with the crash cart.

"She has a living will," said Dee Moreno, RN.

"All right," I replied. "But her son is on the way. We gotta give her a chance."

"She's a DNR," argued Dee.

"I know," I uttered. I turned to Lucy. "Lucy," I yelled at her. She did not move. I made a fist and rubbed my first knuckles across her breastbone. She did not move. "Call a code," I instructed.

"She's a DNR," repeated Dee.

"Call it," I shouted a little too loudly.

The overhead blared, and three more nurses showed up. Lucy did not respond. Her heart rate increased for less than a minute then began to dwindle down again. Down to fifty beats per minute.

"Her heart is giving out," commented Amy Jordan, RN.

Lucy's heart rate dropped to thirty-four.

"She's going, Doc," said Amy.

"I know," I responded tensely.

Lucy opened her eyes and looked straight at me. "It ain't so bad, Doc," she croaked. Then her eyes drifted to the left, and she stared far off across my right shoulder. "Charlie?"

Then the monitor went from thirty-four beats per minute to flatline. Her eyes remained open, but the stare was gone. I took a deep breath.

"She's gone, Doc," stated Amy softly.

"Yes," I responded. I looked at the clock on the wall. "Time of death, thirteen twenty-three." I turned to Amy. "She died on Christmas Eve."

"Can you think of a better time to meet the Lord?" Amy responded quietly.

I walked out of the room and walked slowly to the doctor's dictation room. I sat heavily in the padded chair and dictated the death summary. I then typed a quick note on the computer chart and closed it—closed Lucy's life. I sat there for several minutes.

I walked out to the nurse's desk with slumped shoulders. "Let the funeral home know," I told the ward clerk.

I heard the soft squish of rubber wheelchair tires crunching across the tiled floor. I looked at Michael. He was white haired with a well-trimmed white beard.

"Dr. Holland?" said Michael as he held his right hand out toward me.

I took the muscled, calloused hand and shook it. "Michael?"

"Yes, sir," he responded. "I finally made it. Interstate was a little icy coming over the pass between Laramie and Cheyenne, but it wasn't bad."

"Good," I responded. Michael looked at me expectantly. "Come with me." I motioned down the hall. I walked beside the wheelchair, and we both remained silent. I reached the closed door to Lucy's room. There

I stopped. "Michael, I am afraid your mother died about"—I looked at my watch—"an hour ago."

Michael leaned his head back and looked at the ceiling. "I had hoped to be able to talk to her."

"I am sorry. She died quickly and without any pain."

"Did she say anything?" asked Michael.

"She asked for you. She mentioned Pearl," I said.

"Did she say anything else?" he questioned.

I thought about that for several long seconds. What good would there be in telling about the brake lines? "No. That is all she said. The funeral home should be here soon to pick her up, but you can go in to see her now, if you wish."

"No, I'll wait," he responded. "I think I'll drive out to the old place to see it again."

"As far as I can tell, it is yours now—or will be soon," I remarked. "I don't think there are any other relatives."

"Would you like to drive out there with me?" Michael asked. "If you are not too busy."

"Sure. I'll go with you," I said.

We drove out in his special van, which was set up for his wheelchair. The accelerator and brake were handled by hand. I sat in the front beside him.

"Your mother had a border collie," I stated. "When she got so sick, I adopted him. If you want him back, he is at my house."

"No, Doc. Keep the dog." Michael grinned.

We reached the ranch with no further conversation. The snow on the ground was heaped into drifts by the constant wind.

"Your mother kept talking about the horse out here," I remarked.

"I didn't think she had any horses here," stated Michael.

"So the local rancher said," I admitted. "But at one time, I thought I saw one."

"Hmmm," grunted Michael.

He pulled up in front of the house.

"I think the snow's too deep for my wheelchair," commented Michael.

"Well, I know a couple of guys that would shovel it for you. And you will need to get some propane for the place—if you want to stay for a while," I offered.

"Yeah. I will get a hotel room for a few days until I can get the place livable. I might stay awhile," mused Michael. "At least till after the funeral."

He put the van in drive and started around the loop. I looked out the window at the cute little house. It looked lonely. Then my sight was drawn to two sets of hoofprints stamped in the snow beside the house. Two sets made by two horses. I stayed silent as we drove away.

T HIS IS MY story—although it is really her story. It is a love story, it is a family story, it is a history.

Thus begins the story of the life of Lucy Johansson Morgan. She is a wife, a mother, a businesswoman, a rancher, and a student of life. The story follows her trip through the Great Depression, World War II, Vietnam, and into the third millennium. It tells of her trials and victories, of her gains and losses. She is a determined woman of the Wild West with a surprising strength.

This book is written by Jim Hawley, who is an ER doctor in Wheatland, Wyoming. He has a horse ranch with twenty-eight horses, ten dogs, several cats, and two goats.

CPSIA information can be obtained at www.ICGtesting.com
Printed in the USA
LVOW041832101212

310961LV00006B/958/P